Painting *with* Thread

Painting with Thread

Kit Nicol

COLLINS & BROWN

For Peter, our children and their children – with love.

First published in Great Britain in 2000
by Collins & Brown Limited
64 Brewery Road
London N7 9NT

A member of Chrysalis Books plc

Distributed in the United States and Canada by Sterling Publishing Co,
387 Park Avenue South, New York, NY 10016, USA

1 3 5 7 9 8 6 4 2

British Library Cataloguing-in-Publication Data:
A catalogue record for this book is available from the British Library.

ISBN 1-84340-074-X (paperback)

Editorial Director: Sarah Hoggett
Designer: Claire Graham
Editors: Catherine Ward and Katie Hardwicke
Consultant: Maggi McCormick Gordon
Photographer: Matthew Ward
Illustrators: Coral Mula and Kate Simunek

Reproduction by Global Colour, Malaysia
Printed and bound by Craft Print International Ltd, Singapore

Contents

Introduction

Looking back over the years, I realize that I have always been fascinated by many aspects of artistic creativity – drawing, painting, stitching and embroidery – experimenting both with the usual as well as the unusual in an endeavour to create images and subjects that are pleasing to the eye. This led me to question the possibility of combining a variety of visual art forms to produce a further development of the traditional painted picture.

I found that a really rewarding effect could be achieved by creating a picture which, from a distance, has the appearance of a painting but on close inspection reveals the intricacies and three-dimensional texture of stitches. The rich embossed surfaces that the needle can create are really exciting when combined and contrasted with the smooth harmonizing qualities of traditional watercolour painting.

I remember well my first, small thread painting and the thrill of discovering that the mark-making qualities of both stitch and watercolour could be of equal value visually.

I already had a great appreciation of fabric and threads, and the pleasure of handling and using them in their abundant variety. I also enjoyed the contrasts – on the one hand the joy of stitchery and the rhythm of the needle as it passed through the fabric, and on the other the very different, instant quality of the fluid watercolour painting – so why not combine the two methods in one pictorial concept?

Through my examples and step-by-step instructions, I hope to share some of the pleasure and experience of painting with threads. It is a stimulating medium with great potential, waiting to be discovered in your own individual way.

Kit Nicol

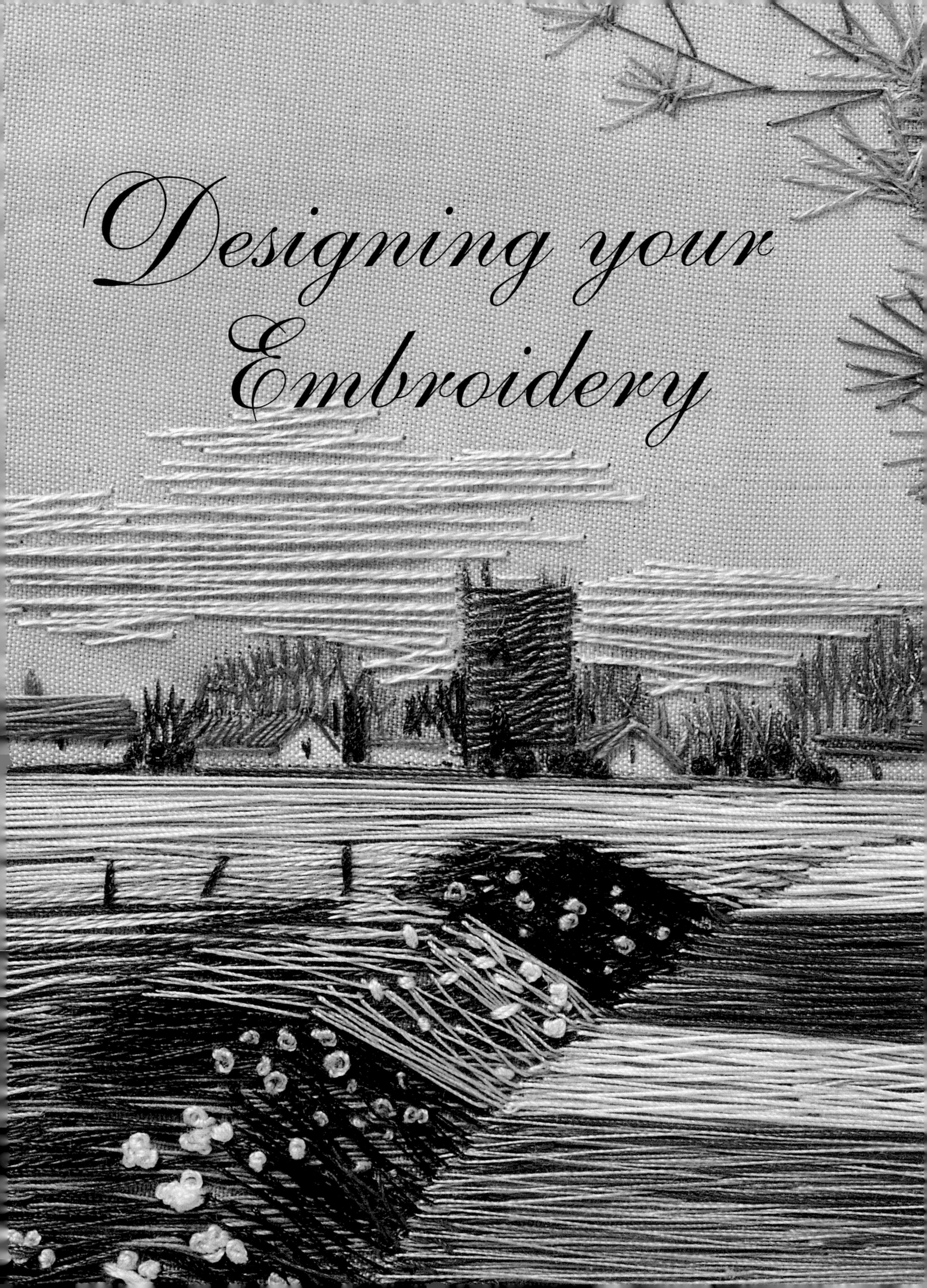

Designing your Embroidery

Inspiration

My usual source of inspiration is observing nature. A country walk can provide a wealth of information, and I usually carry a small sketchbook and a pencil to record scenes that attract me. If you find a blank sheet of paper and the idea of 'design' daunting, take a camera and snap things that interest you, so you can browse through them at leisure later. Take pictures when you travel and on holiday, and use them in the same way to create a piece of work that will remind you of a favourite scene or event.

I turn to flowers again and again in my work. If floral subjects interest you, too, try using paintings and photos as well as the real thing to provide source material. As well as using flowers as single subjects, I also use them as part of larger compositions such as a corner of my garden.

Family photographs, particularly those of children, can provide a wealth of ideas and inspiration. A personal interpretation that is a unique gift today can become a family heirloom to pass on and give enormous pleasure to future generations.

A favourite object can be reproduced in its entirety or used as part of a larger composition. Let your own taste and inherent originality direct you and help you make choices.

Flowers

There are countless books and magazines with botanical images that can be adapted to create beautiful thread paintings. Seed catalogues, postcards and greetings cards all offer references that can be collected and used at a later date.

Sketches

I always carry a sketchbook with me and find that even quick sketches, or notes, can be very useful when I come to planning an embroidered picture. If you don't feel confident with a pencil and sketchbook, take photographs instead.

Photographs

Snaps of familiar places, as nearby as your own back garden, or photos of exotic holiday locations, are equally valid as source material for thread paintings.

Favourite objects

Any number of motifs can be picked up from a simple everyday object like this serving platter, and adapted for use.

Family Portraits

People, and especially children, can be a wonderful source of inspiration for charming cameo portraits. You do not need to achieve an exact likeness, but use favourite objects, toys or clothes that you associate with someone's character. My granddaughter, Grace, loved her pink bicycle, so I pictured her riding it with her toy duck in the basket.

Grace's favourite toy has been recreated in stumpwork (see page 29).

The bicycle frame is made of wrapped wires and the wheel covers are pink leather.

Planning your Painting

Once you have decided upon the subject of your thread painting, take some time to put your ideas on to paper, aiming to work out balanced forms to create pleasing patterns.

If you are planning a landscape or seasape, consider making a few thumbnail sketches of the scene. You can eliminate any unwanted detail at this stage, concentrating on the features that appeal. Look for patterns and textures that you could recreate in thread and make notes on colours to assist your memory. Use sketches or photographs as reminders. Try to simplify the scene into clear, flat shapes.

Decide on the format for the picture (see box, right) and consider the finer points of the composition (see pages 14–15) before you draw your final sketch ready to transfer to the fabric (see page 25).

Reference material

Once you have found your source of inspiration, make some detailed sketches of all the elements that appeal to you. Take some photographs as reference and use them to help you combine your favourite features into one idea. Make a thumbnail sketch to simplify the main shapes. You can use this to make templates to transfer the finished design to fabric (see page 25).

Choosing a Format

There are three main formats to choose from: square, portrait and landscape. Square format is self-contained and balanced. Portrait format lends itself to tall subjects or those with detailed foregrounds. Landscape format naturally suits a landscape subject and allows you to include a large expanse of sky.

Portrait format

Square format

Landscape format

Colour notes

Before you start work on your painting, you may find it useful to make notes about the type of stitches, any embellishments and the colours that you plan to use. Annotate your sketches and experiment with paint colours and different combinations of thread colours before you start.

Gold paint has been used as part of the design.

A sketch annotated with paint colours is a useful reference when applying the paint to your embroidery.

Composition

Unless you intend your embroidery to be of an isolated subject, such as a flower or a figure, you will need to compose the picture carefully to achieve a pleasing effect and to focus attention on the main theme of your thread painting.

Start by deciding the position of the horizon, and your point of interest: this often looks better when placed off-centre to achieve an irregular balance. A device often used by artists to organize the picture areas is to envisage it divided into thirds (see below).

Rule of Thirds

You can either mentally superimpose a grid of thirds over your planned picture, or draw one out to help you plan your composition. Place key elements of your picture at the intersections of the grid and use vertical and horizontal lines as guides for positioning other features, such as the horizon or a tall figure. In the painting *Gone Fishing* (right), the high horizon follows the top third, whilst the figure of the fisherman on the left is almost aligned on a vertical third.

Low horizon

A low horizon gives you space to include a large expanse of sky – ideal for cloud studies. It gives an open feel to the image.

High horizon

A high horizon allows you to include a lot of detail in the foreground and gives an enclosed and intimate feel to the picture.

Focal point

You can use elements of your picture to direct attention to your chosen point of interest. Diagonal lines are very useful: for example, the path in the painting Formal Garden *(right), leads diagonally from the bottom of the picture to the fountain and rose arch. The pale colour of the path contrasts with the surrounding garden and also helps to focus attention on the fountain.*

The path breaks the bottom edge of the picture and leads up to the fountain.

The three-dimensional urn in the foreground balances the picture.

Compositional devices

In this painting, several compositional devices have been used to direct attention to the distant windmill. A high horizon gives plenty of room to add foreground detail and texture. The use of warm colours in the foreground and cool colours in the background creates a sense of space and depth.

The windmill is placed in the middle-ground, off-centre.

The shoreline meanders across the picture, leading the eye to the distant windmill.

Using Colour

The world is full of wonderful colours, but it can be bewildering to a novice thread painter. Simplification can be of great value, and I use a limited palette, intermixing three primary hues, when I am painting in watercolour. I then select from an abundance of thread colours for the stitching. To use colour successfully you need to follow a few simple rules to combine and use colour to good effect. I have devised a floral colour wheel (below), to help to explain colour theory.

Think about pairing complementary colours to create a strong effect, or combining harmonious shades for subtle changes. Contrasting colours will give immediate impact.

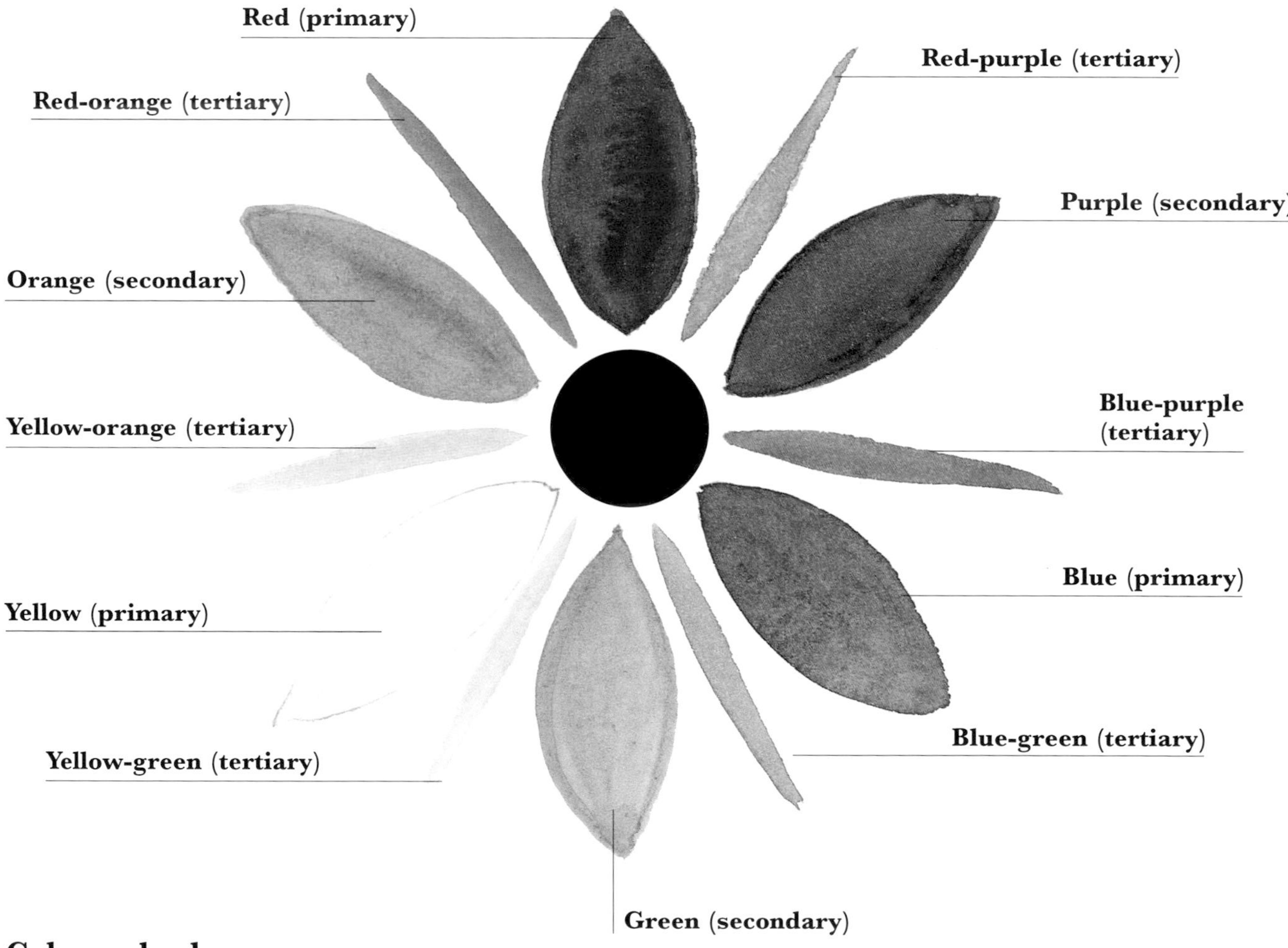

Colour wheel

The colour wheel shows the relationship of the basic colours. When two primary colours (red, yellow or blue) are mixed they produce secondaries. A tertiary is mixed from a secondary and its adjacent primary. You can achieve neutral colours, such as grey, beige and brown by combining the primaries in varying proportions.

Colour Combinations

Careful colour combinations can have an immediate impact. Many successful combinations occur in nature – look at flower petals and leaves for inspiration.

Complementary

Complementary colours appear opposite one another on the colour wheel and add dramatic impact and 'sparkle' to your embroidery.

Red

Green

Yellow

Purple

Blue

Orange

Harmonious

Harmonious colours are those adjacent to each other on the colour wheel. A range of tones between these colours, for example from blue to purple, will give a gentle transition. This can be achieved by using different shades of thread or mixing your paint colours.

Contrasting colours

Contrast is paramount in working with colour. Unless there are differences of tone – light and dark – your pictures will be bland, and you need variations in the shading to make some elements stand out and others recede into the background.

The juxtaposition of yellow and green adds accent to the colour scheme.

Pictorial Effects

An infinite variety of pictorial effects can be created in thread paintings. One important aspect is texture – the surface quality of the picture – which can be experienced visually as well as by touch. The type and size of thread, the density of the stitching, and the use of colour all have a dynamic impact on texture, and the use of embellishment, from interior padding to beads and sequins, also plays a part. Also consider the effects of perspective and light and shade, to give your embroideries depth and form that resembles similar effects achieved by artists in other media.

Water

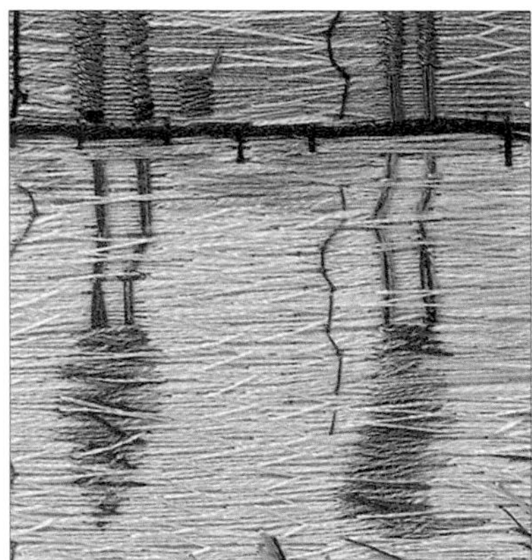

Reflections
Water is never still and images reflected in the water are vague in colour and outline. A few light-blue Cretan stitches worked over the reflection give a rippled, muted effect.

Falling water
Droplets of water in a fountain or waterfall should be recreated not as a solid line but with small individual stitches, spaced according to the force of the spray and the distance from the viewer.

Ripples
In order to look convincing, ripples on the surface of the water must follow the outline and direction of the moving object that is creating them. Ripples will be more prominent in the foreground.

Light and Shade

Visual texture depends heavily on a depiction of light and shadow, which can be achieved both through the density of stitches and a careful choice of colours – the same flower seen in sunshine will be a different hue if it is in shadow. Remember also that colours appear paler and cooler as they recede into the distance.

Light on water

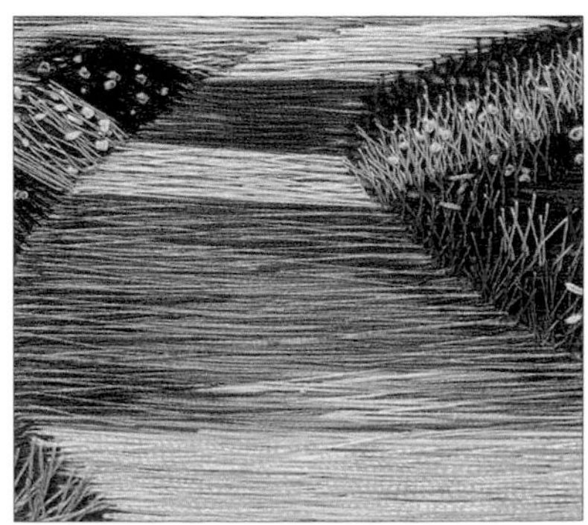

Shadows

TEXTURE

Sequins and beads

Myriad objects can be used to give surface texture, among them sequins and beads, which add sparkle and flashes of light. Sequins and beads make excellent flower centres as well as eyes and ornaments, and can often work well instead of French knots.

Density

The size, length and density of the stitches themselves, as well as the type and colour of the threads used, create texture. Heavier weight threads will appear closer than finer ones.

French knots

French knots are amongst the most useful of all embroidery stitches for creating texture. They can be used individually to make flower centres or eyes, or massed together to make banks of flowers, the wool on a lamb or a child's hair.

Mass

The mass of a tree or shrub in leaf can be depicted in a number of ways, using different-coloured blocks of horizontal, vertical or diagonal Cretan stitch radiating from a central point. You can also use filling stitches such as seeding and French knots.

Figures

People can be worked using a variety of techniques, from simple, surface stitches to padded and wired bodies covered with intricate needlelace garments. It is essential to keep body proportions accurate to achieve a realistic effect.

Animals

Animals can be stylized into simplified shapes that can look remarkably life-like, and can be stitched as surface motifs or padded and overstitched. Cretan stitch and straight stitch both create a realistic fur effect, and birds and insects can be made in needlelace.

Painting and Embroidery Techniques

Materials

The fabric used for thread painting should be, above all, easy and enjoyable to stitch. I use silk because it gives the best pure colour and luminosity to the painted backgrounds on which my work is based. I use good-quality, even-weave dress fabric and usually work on white, off-white or cream. A stronger tone may affect the colour – possibly both actual and perceived – of the paints you use.

All silk fabrics will need to be backed with muslin (cheesecloth) to provide extra strength to take the stitches. Cotton can be used for backing trapunto, and felt and wadding (batting) for padding shapes.

The choice of threads for embroidery is endless: sewing thread, knitting yarn, crochet cotton, chenille and cord, and of course conventional and novelty embroidery threads, can all be incorporated.

Fabric and threads

The range of threads available for embroidery is too wide to do more than mention the most popular here. You will also need a selection of silk fabrics to stitch onto, together with cotton or muslin (cheesecloth) for backing.

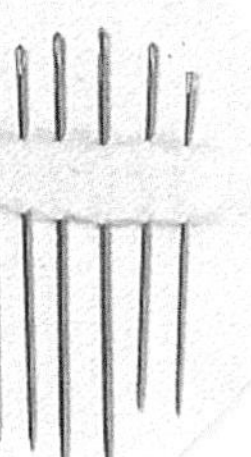

Needles – assorted sharps

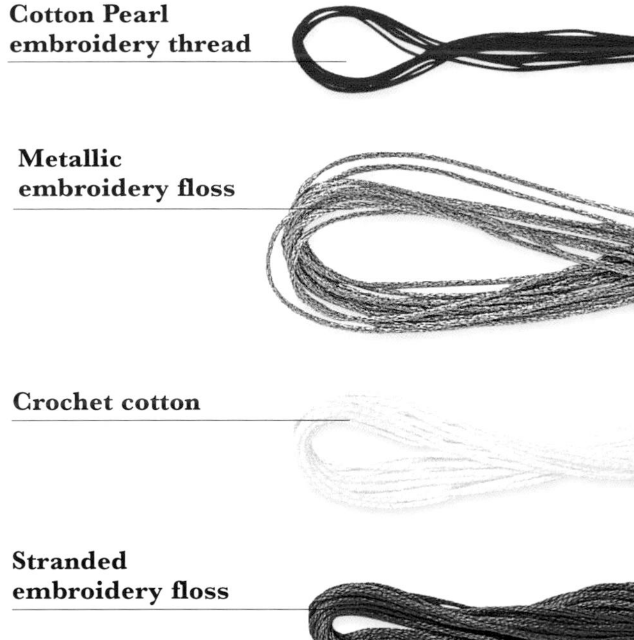

Cotton Pearl embroidery thread

Metallic embroidery floss

Crochet cotton

Stranded embroidery floss

Embroidery cotton

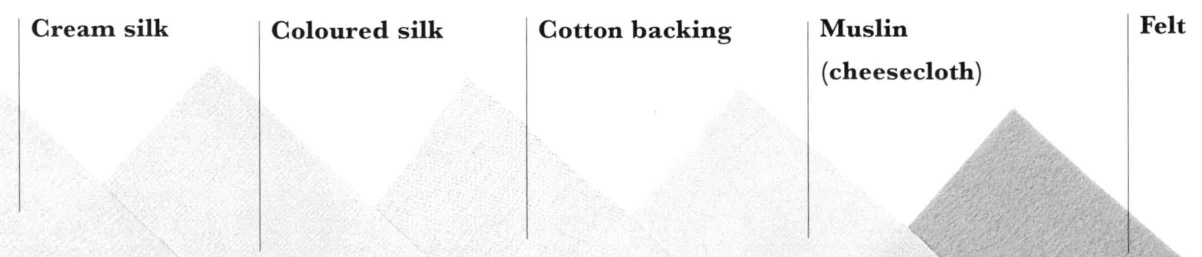

Cream silk

Coloured silk

Cotton backing

Muslin (cheesecloth)

Felt

Embellishments and trimmings

Any trimming or 3-D object that can be attached to a picture in some way can be used, with beads, sequins, ribbon and lace among the most useful and easily available.

Wadding (batting)

Ribbon

Coloured glass beads

Black sequins

Glass beads

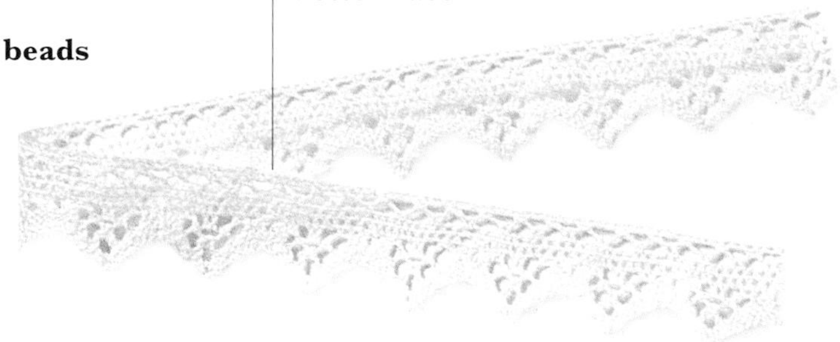

Cotton lace

Long beads

Metallic beads

Pearls

Florist's medium-gauge wire

Preparing a Frame

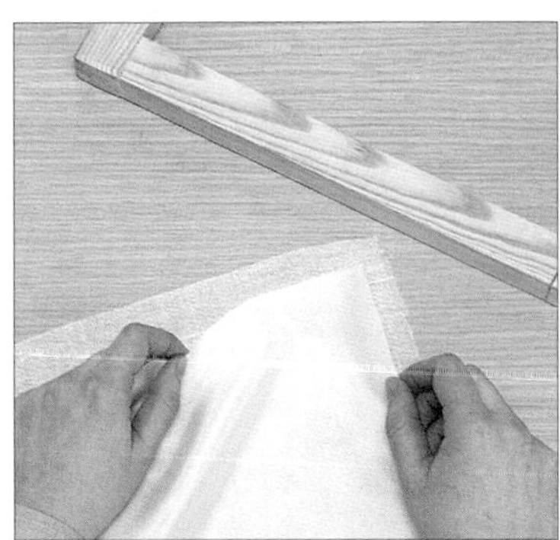

1 Cut pieces of silk and muslin 5 cm (2 in) larger than the outer edge of the frame, all round. Line up the straight grain on both fabrics.

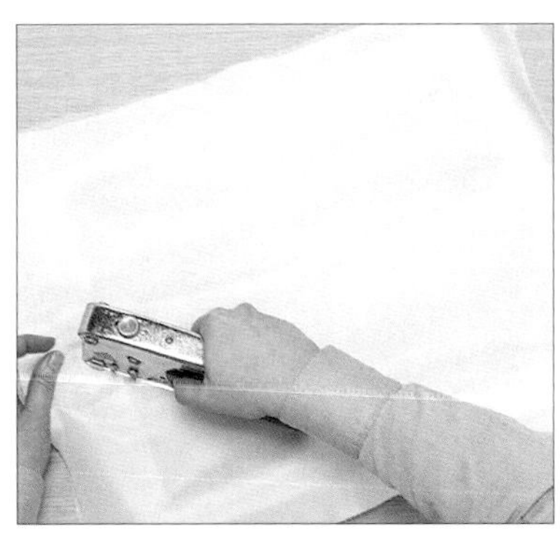

2 Staple the fabrics to the centre of one side of the frame, then stretch it taut and staple on the opposite side.

3 Work out towards the corner of the frame, stretching and stapling on opposite sides and keeping the fabric taut. The frame is now ready to use.

Getting Started

You will only need a few basic art materials for painting your fabric. Good-quality art brushes are a joy to use. I prefer to use tubes of pure watercolour paint and find that I can achieve a wonderful array of colours from mixing the three primary hues.

You will need a large white palette to mix your colours – a few saucers or white plates will do. Always have clean water to hand. I use one pot to wash out dirty brushes and one to pick up clean water when mixing new colours.

You can use several different methods to transfer your finished composition to your prepared fabric – draw directly on to the prepared surface with pencil (your marks will be covered by paint and embroidery stitches) or draw around templates. Alternatively, trace your design and use the carbon transfer method.

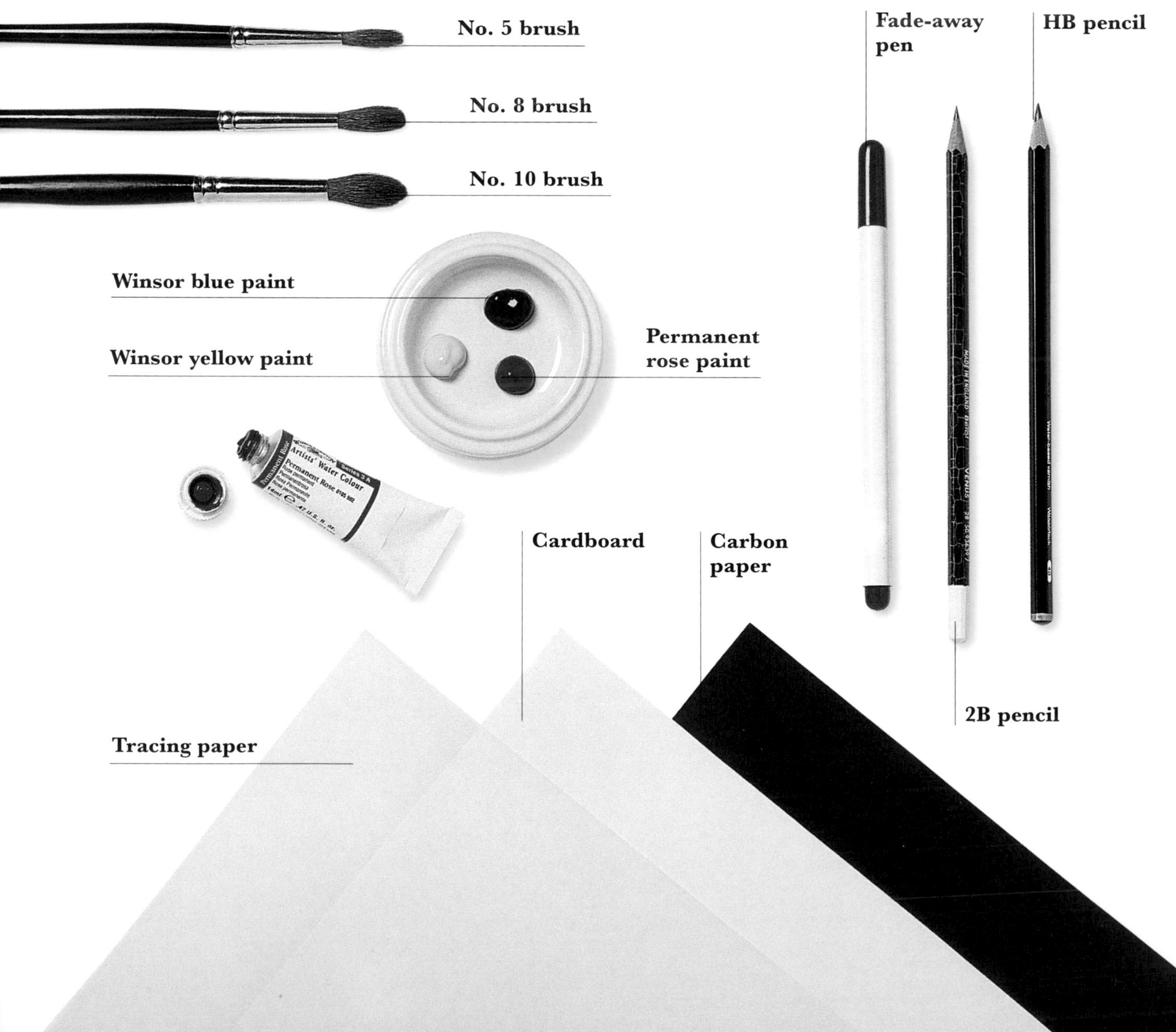

Tracing and Carbon Transfer

1 Enlarge or reduce the image or sketch to the size of your finished embroidery. Place tracing paper over the image and trace the main outlines.

2 Place a sheet of carbon paper between the tracing and the silk fabric. With an HB pencil, carefully draw over the outlines on the tracing paper.

3 Remove the tracing paper and the carbon paper to reveal the transferred pattern beneath. The fabric is now ready to be painted and stitched.

Using Templates

1 Draw the main shapes of your picture on to a piece of stiff card, the same size as your finished embroidery. Cut out the shapes to make card templates.

2 Place the templates on the silk fabric, following your composition. Draw around each template with an HB pencil.

3 The pencil outlines of the main elements of the picture can now be used as a guide for painting and embroidery stitches.

Using a Fade-away Pen

Fade-away, or magic, pens are available from craft shops. You can use them to draw directly on to the silk, or to trace around templates. The pen-mark will eventually disappear, making it ideal for designs that are worked in pale-coloured threads. Test the time limit of the pen on a spare scrap of the same fabric first.

Painting

You can use paint as much or as little as you like. Spend some time mixing different combinations of my selection of three basic colours to see the enormous variety of tints and shades that are possible. Always try out your colour on a spare piece of the same fabric before committing it to your prepared silk, as some fabrics react differently to paint.

Controlling watercolour paint needs practice but the effects are very exciting. You will soon become familiar with the proportions of water to paint needed to achieve the required consistency. If painting is new to you, experiment first with a single-colour wash. Remember to mix your colours slightly darker than the desired shade as the paint will dry lighter.

Basic Colours

Below are a few examples of the different colours that can be mixed from just the three primary hues.

Permanent rose

Winsor blue

Winsor yellow

Suggestions for skies

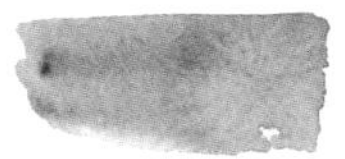

Winsor blue and Winsor yellow

Winsor blue and permanent rose

Permanent rose and Winsor yellow

Suggestions for flowers and leaves

Winsor blue and Winsor yellow

Winsor blue and permanent rose

Permanent rose and Winsor yellow

Suggestions for stonework

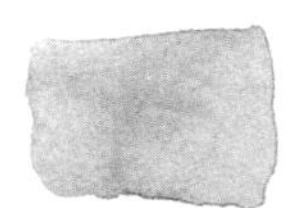

Permanent rose and Winsor yellow, touch of Winsor blue

Permanent rose and Winsor yellow

Winsor blue and Winsor yellow, touch of permanent rose

Mixing Colours on Fabric

Watercolour washes blend together on the fabric to give a gentle transition from one colour to another. This method is useful when painting backgrounds – to achieve a sense of distance and perspective, a colour can be made paler. The colours will diffuse and spread of their own accord, merging gently together. The gradation of tone dries to give a soft, hazy quality of light, ideal for a sky study.

Painting a Single-colour Sky Wash

An effective sky wash can be achieved with a single-colour mix diluted with water.

Winsor blue

Diluted wash

1 Dilute the paint with water. Test the intensity of the wash on spare piece of fabric. Load your brush with the wash and lay the first stroke across the top of the fabric.

2 Work quickly from left to right across the fabric, diluting the intensity of the wash as you approach the horizon line.

Painting a Cloud

Using a single-colour wash, you can create simple cloud shapes by painting around a cloud template.

Diluted Winsor blue mixed with a touch of permanent rose

1 Draw a cumulous cloud shape on to stiff card and cut out to make a template. Paint around the edge of the template.

2 When the template is removed you will have the soft outline of a cloud. Fill in the sky with a diluted wash.

Painting Fine Details

Use a fairly dry brush for details, and one with a fine point on the end to give you more control for drawing.

Permanent rose mixed with Winsor blue

1 Mix a suitable colour with a little water. Using the point of a fine brush, such as a no. 5, paint over your pencil outlines.

2 Continue to build up the finer details, using different intensities of colour to give a variety of effects.

3-D Effects

One of the advantages of combining threads with watercolour is the lure of creating three-dimensional effects. The light and shadows created by working in three dimensions, with some areas raised above the surface, however slightly, add greatly to the appeal and interest of the picture.

There are many ways to achieve this effect, from padding the background, to overlaying stitches, or adding embellishments. Some stitches are in themselves three-dimensional, including the needlelace stitches that I use for garments. Wirework is used to effect for items such as chairs, archways and figures.

Trapunto

1 Prepare the background. Cut a piece of thin cotton backing larger than the shape to be padded. *Inset*: Tack (baste) the backing to the wrong side.

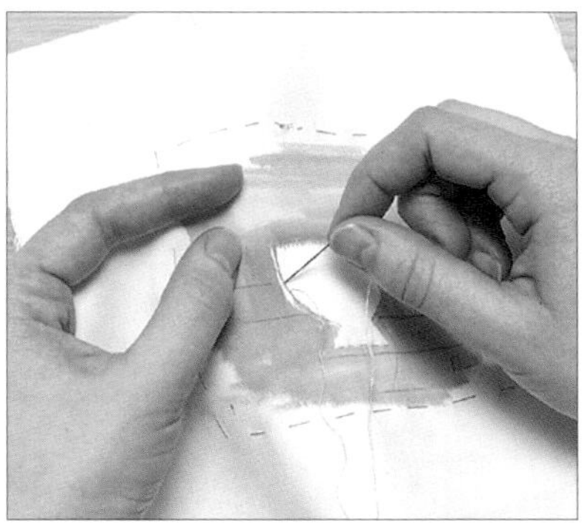

2 Using matching thread, stitch through both layers to outline the shape with running stitch or backstitch.

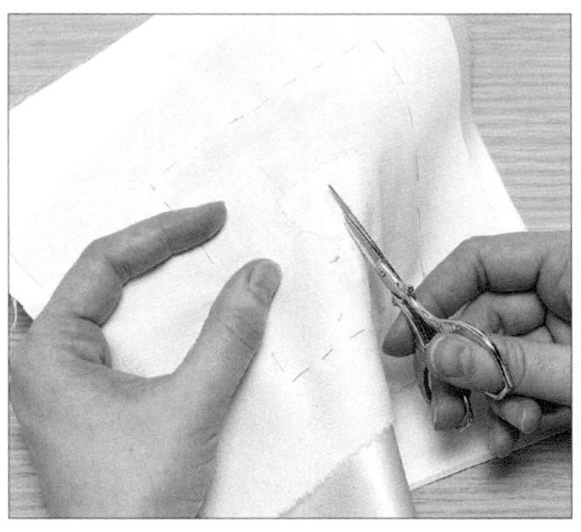

3 Carefully make a small slit *only* in the backing fabric in the centre of the shape.

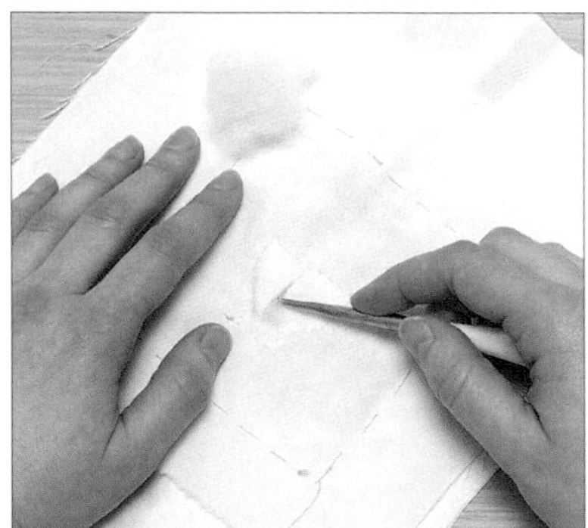

4 Insert stuffing to lightly pad the shape. Use a blunt tool to work a small amount of stuffing into the corners if necessary.

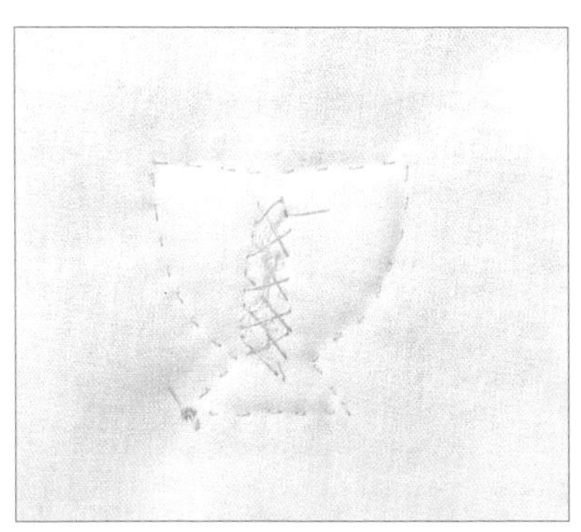

5 Use herringbone stitch to oversew the slit and hold in the stuffing.

6 The finished shape is softly padded and stands out from the background.

Soft Sculpture – Heads

1 Make two oval card templates, one slightly smaller than the other. Cut out a fabric oval using the larger template.

2 Run a gathering stitch all around the fabric oval, sewing close to the edge. Place the smaller template on the wrong side of the fabric oval and gently pull up the gathering thread to make a head shape. Press the edges lightly (with the card template still inside) to make a firm crease, then remove the template.

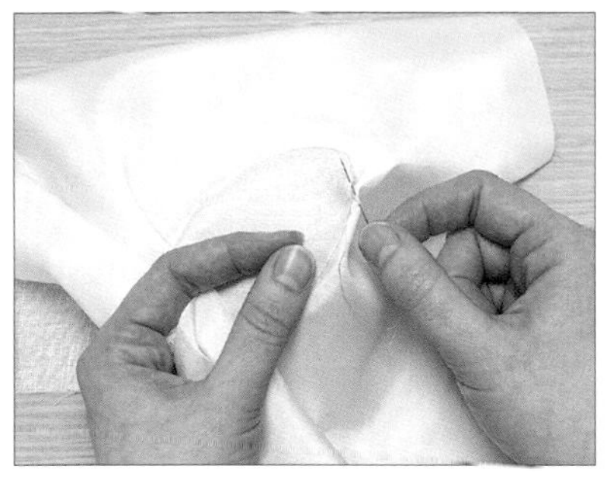

3 Invisibly stitch the head shape to the background fabric, leaving an opening through which to insert the stuffing.

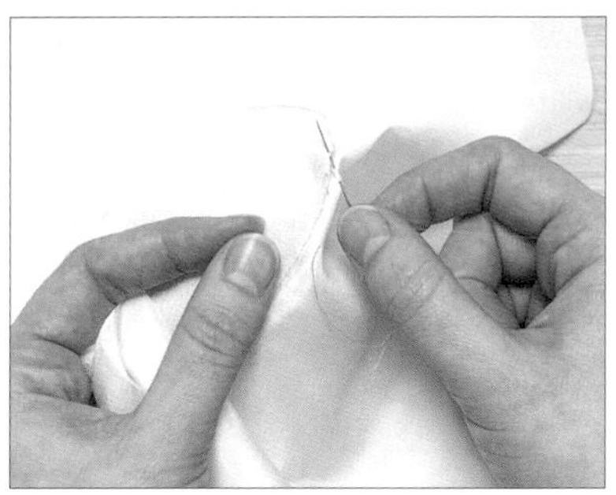

4 Insert small pieces of stuffing to lightly pad the head. Then finish stitching the head shape in place.

5 The finished face is now ready for features or hair to be added.

Stumpwork

1 Cut out three template shapes from felt, each smaller than the one before. If covering wth needlelace, use a colour as close to the chosen thread as possible.

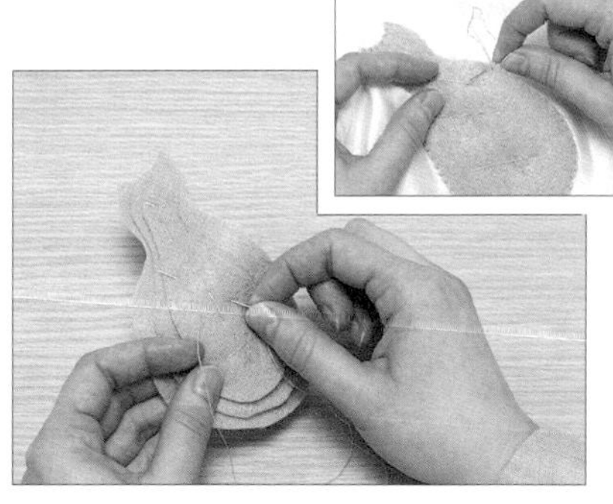

2 Tack (baste) the shapes together, with the smaller shapes centred on the largest one. *Inset:* Turn the shape over, with the largest shape uppermost, and stitch to the right side of the fabric.

3 The padded stumpwork shape now has a soft rounded edge and is ready to be embellished.

Wirework

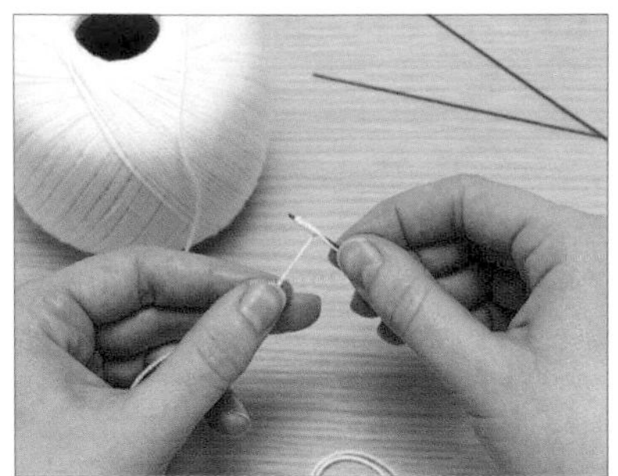

1 Cut the wires to the desired length. Hold one end of cotton along the top of the wire and wrap tightly. Continue wrapping to the end of the wire, and secure with a slip knot.

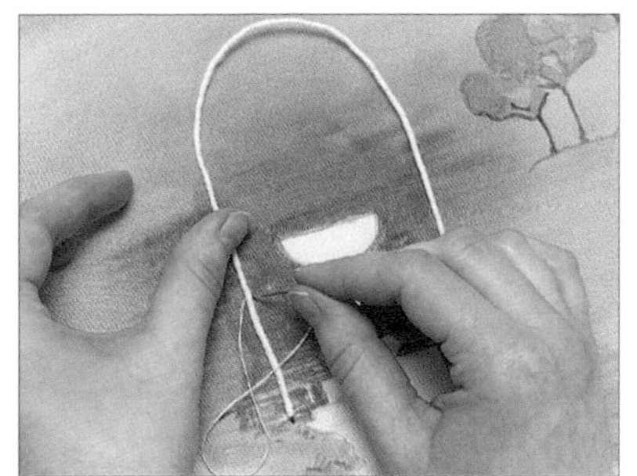

2 Gently bend the wire to the desired shape. Stitch the wire shape to the background using thread to match the colour of the wrapped wire.

3 The finished shape can now be embellished. Make sure the embellishment or embroidery stitches cover the ends of the wires.

Making Wire Hands

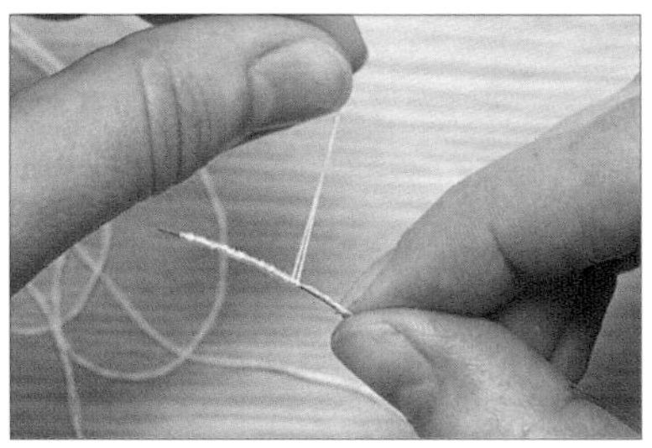

1 Wrap five pieces of fine wire with flesh-coloured thread. Use one or two strands only and wrap lengths of about 5–7 cm (2–2½ in).

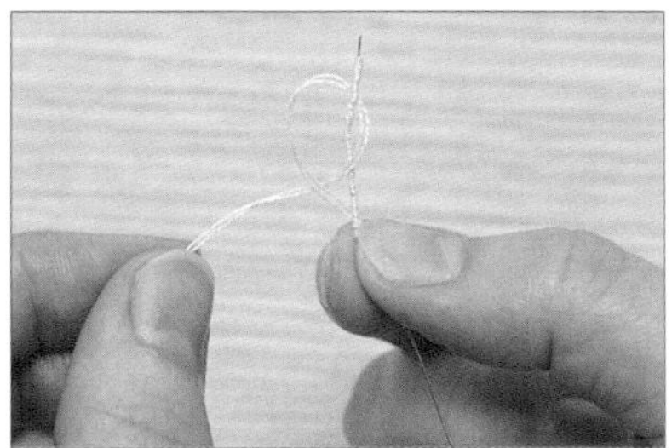

2 Tie off each piece with a slip knot to secure the wrapped threads.

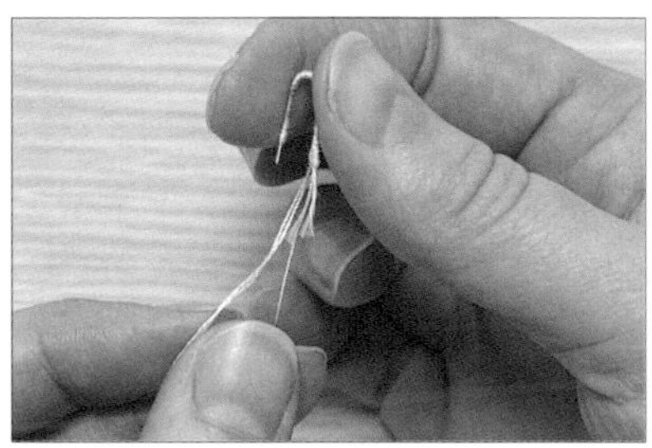

3 Bend each wrapped wire to make the fingers and thumb, and press the bent area together tightly.

4 Arrange four bent wires to make fingers, with the shortest at one side and the longest in the middle. Bind together to cover the wires and loose threads.

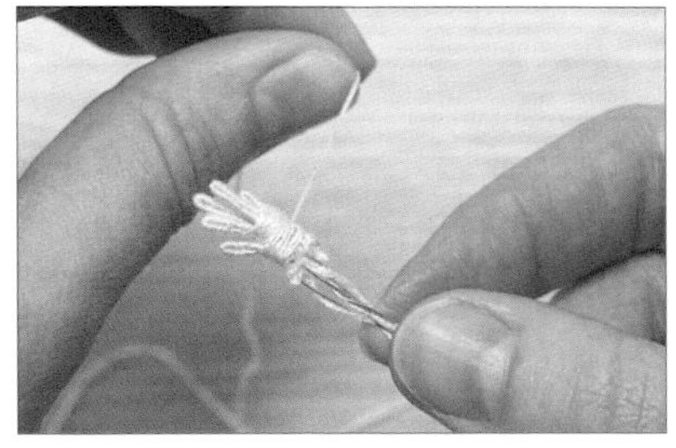

5 Add the fifth bent wire to make the thumb and continue binding the hand to make the wrist.

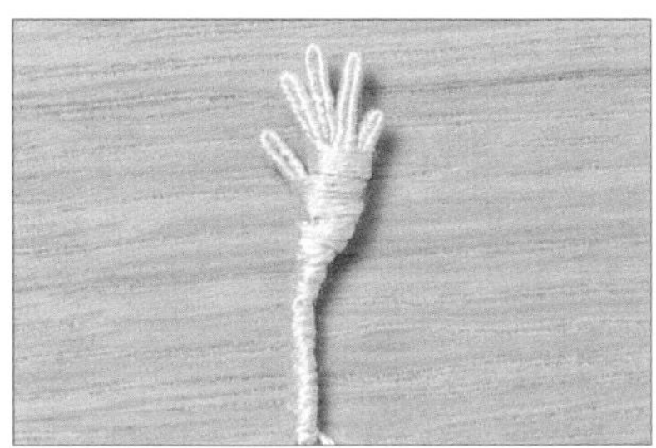

6 Tie the binding thread securely and trim the excess wire and thread to make a finished hand shape.

Making Hair

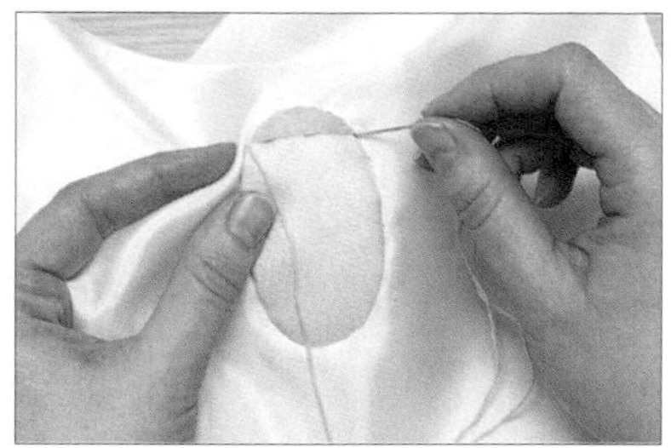

1 Start with an applied face or head shape (see page 29). To make plaits, stitch from one side to the other, starting at the top of the head shape. Continue to the point where the plaits begin.

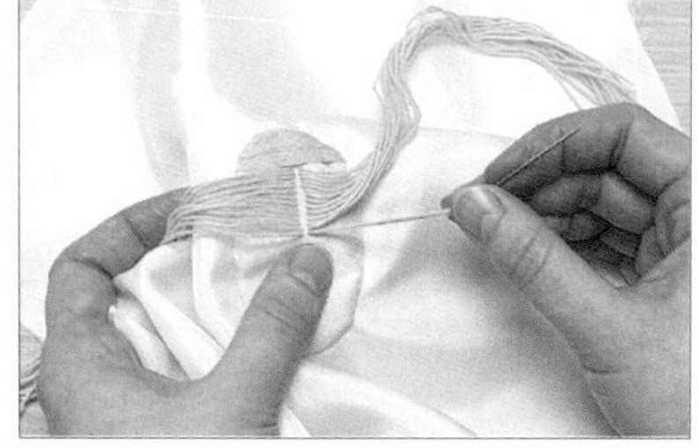

2 Stitch two rows of long loose threads down the back of the head. Tie off each thread at the back of the work, and work alternate sides to keep the threads fairly equal on each side.

3 Fill in the area behind the top of the plaits with matching thread. You will not need a hoop if your fabric is already stretched on a frame.

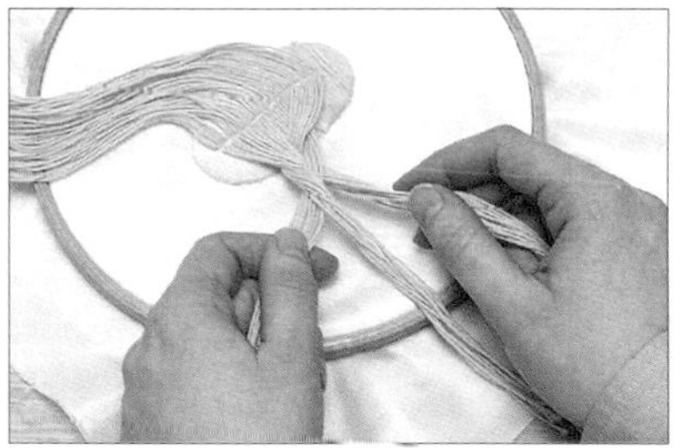

4 Divide each set of long threads into three equal bunches and plait them together.

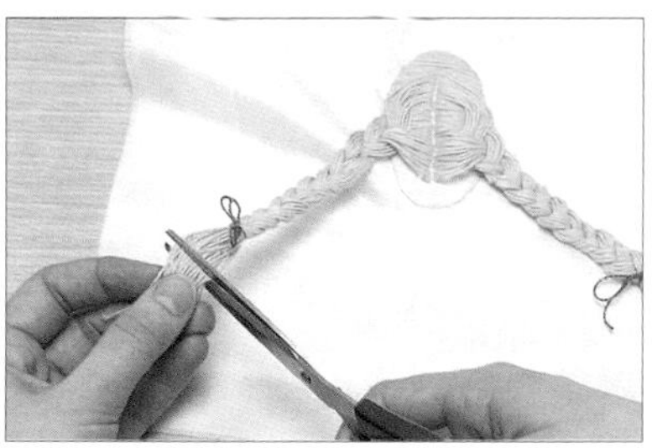

5 Tie the end of each plait with a thread or ribbon and trim the ends of the plaits neatly.

6 The finished plaits can be secured with a few hidden stitches if desired.

Making Arms

1 Cut a piece of florist's medium-gauge wire the same length as the arm. Then cut a rectangle of flesh-coloured felt slightly wider and longer than the wire.

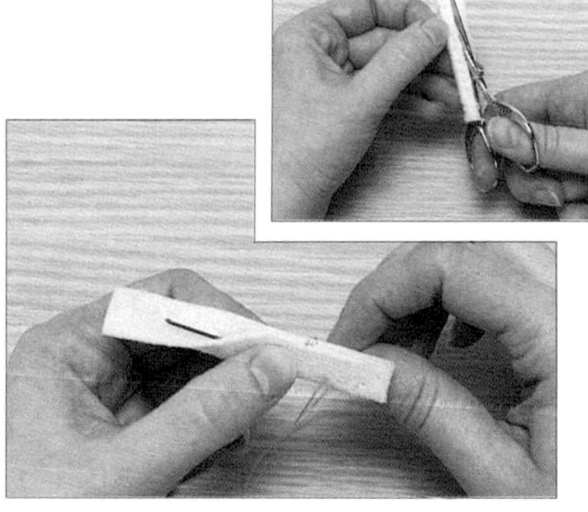

2 Fold the felt in half along the wire. Stitch through both layers of felt next to the wire, using matching thread and a simple stab stitch. *Inset:* Trim the felt close to the seam. Cut a rounded shape at one end for the hand.

3 Using the same thread, make a few straight stitches to represent fingers and thumb. Bend the wire at the 'wrist' and 'elbow' to make the finished arm. For a rounded edge, stitch over the edge of the felt.

Making Needlelace Clothes

1 Cut a paper pattern of the desired shape. Then cut two or three layers of felt template (see Stumpwork, page 29) in a colour to co-ordinate with the chosen threads.

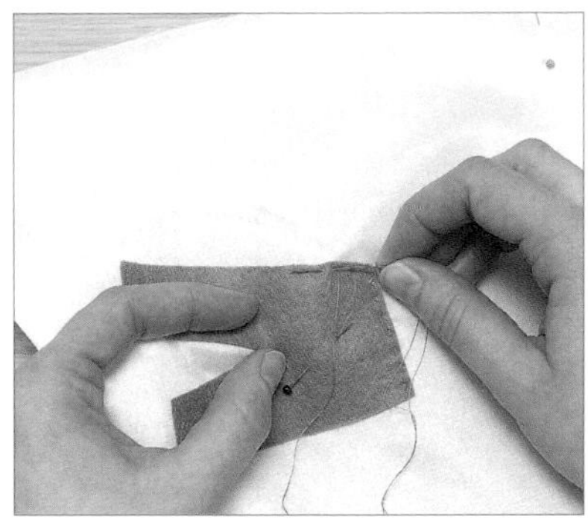

2 Position the felt shapes on the background fabric, using running stitch to sew around the edge. You will not need a hoop if your fabric is already stretched on a frame.

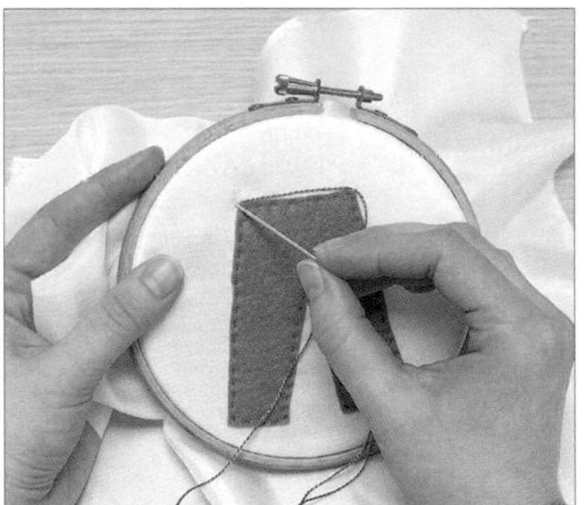

3 Using a long strand of pearl thread, bring the needle up at the top left-hand corner and through to the back in the opposite corner. Repeat in the opposite direction.

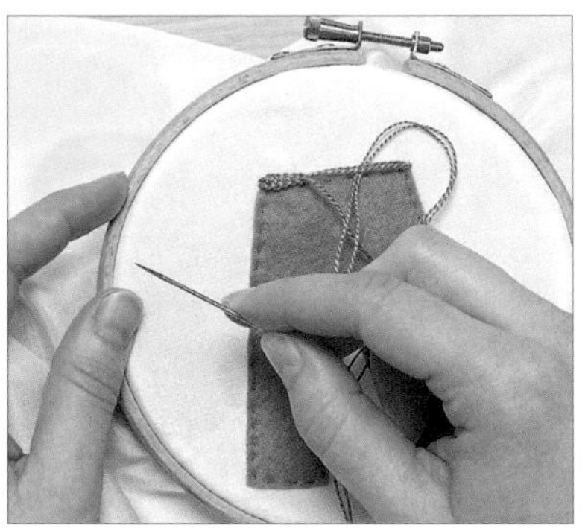

4 Using the same length of thread, make a row of buttonhole loops (see page 43) along the two laid threads.

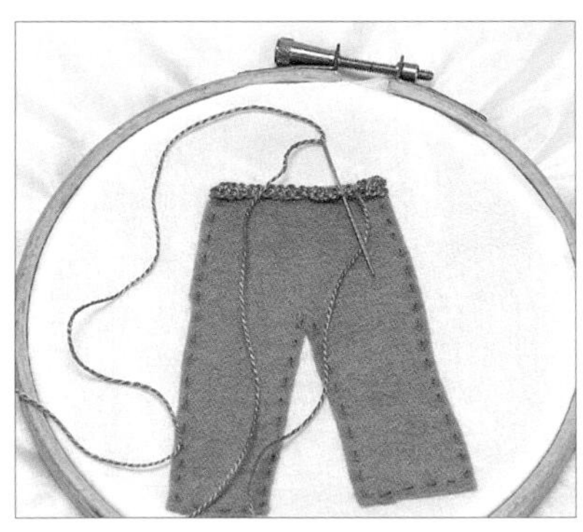

5 Work alternate rows of buttonhole loops over the laid thread in opposite directions, working into the loops of the row above.

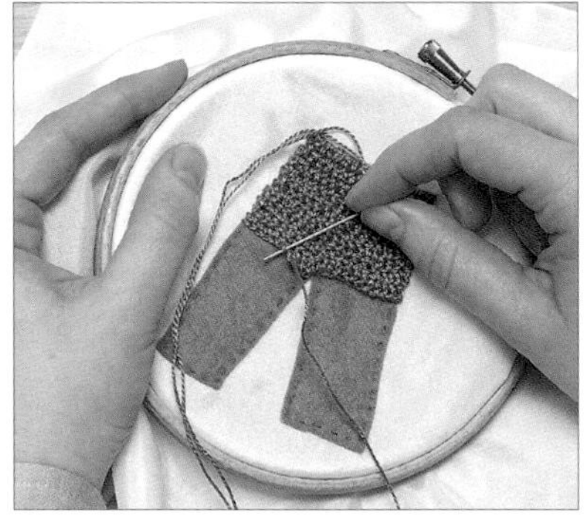

6 Continue working alternate rows of buttonhole loops until you reach a point where the shape divides, then work in the same way down one side to the bottom of the shape.

7 Work down the second side of the shape using the same method. Leave the rows loose so that feet and shoes can be inserted as desired. The finished trousers (right) cover the felt shape completely.

Framing

Once your thread painting is complete, you will want to display it. You can, of course, take your painting to be professionally framed, or follow the simple method below if you wish to use a ready-made frame and mount. Think carefully about the colour of the mount as strong colours can overpower a picture. Neutral creams and greys are subtle and will set-off the picture to good effect.

You can cut the mount yourself, or even make one from a simply quilted or stitched piece of fabric, mounted on to board and placed over your embroidery.

1 Carefully remove the embroidery from the frame. Pad the picture with two layers of soft fabric or blotting paper, then stretch the silk on to the centre of a 3-ply board. Staple in place.

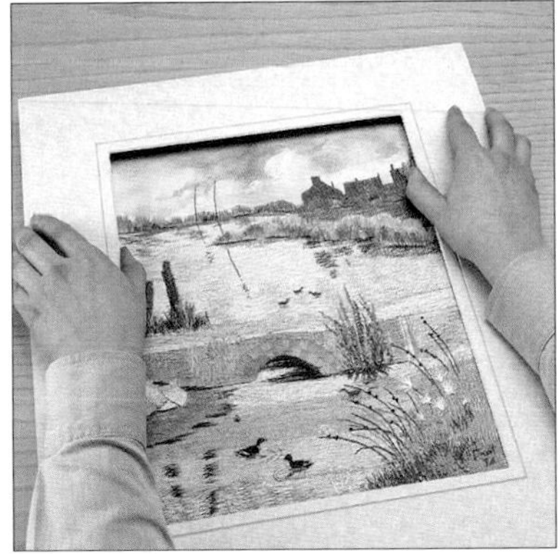

2 Place a cardboard mount (in a harmonizing colour and cut to the same size as the backing board) over the picture.

3 The thread painting is now ready to be framed.

Quilted Frames

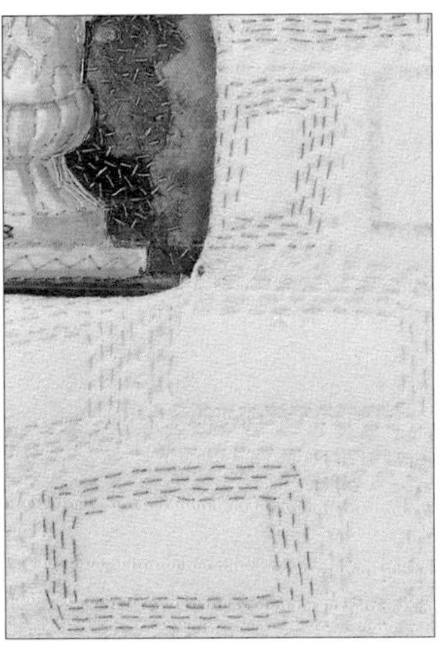

You can finish your thread painting by continuing the embroidery theme on to the mount. Cut a card mount with a shaped aperture if you wish. Cut a piece of silk fabric and wadding (batting) to the same size as the card, and trim away the central area allowing a seam of 2.5 cm (1 in). Tack (baste) the wadding and fabric together and quilt. Glue the finished fabric to the mount, turning the central seam under.

Kit

Stitch Library

Stitches

Most of the stitches used to make the projects in this book are variations on well-known embroidery stitches. The instructions included here illustrate how to work the stitches used in the projects on pages 50–123, giving you the regular, traditional method followed by an irregular variation where appropriate. By working stitches of random lengths and alternating directions, you can achieve a gallery of different effects, or you can try your own favourite stitches.

Even if you are new to embroidery, you can still achieve a detailed and successful thread painting using just two or three simple embroidery stitches, such as Cretan stitch (page 42) and irregular straight stitch (page 37). For added detail and texture experiment with stitches such as padded satin stitch (page 40) and French knots (page 41). Many of the clothes that are used to dress the figures in some of the thread paintings are made from needlelace stitches, these are all based on buttonhole stitch variations (page 43).

Before you start stitching, think carefully about the colours of thread that you plan to use (see page 16). To prevent part-skeins and leftover ends from becoming tangled, wrap them around acid-free cardboard or plastic bobbins, and label them with a colour reference number. Organize your threads by colour and store in clear plastic bags, either by project or by colour family (see page 16).

Many embroiderers prefer to use a hoop when working, but the scale of these projects and the combination of painting and needlework prevents the use of small devices. I find that the wooden frame (see page 23) provides a sturdy framwork for working stitches and keeps the fabric taut.

Stitching and painting are both absorbing pastimes and you should consider your working position before you start. Make sure that you are sitting comfortably and take regular breaks to avoid repetitive strain injury. Ensure that you are working in a good light: a daylight bulb or magnifying lamp is a good investment.

Threading a Needle

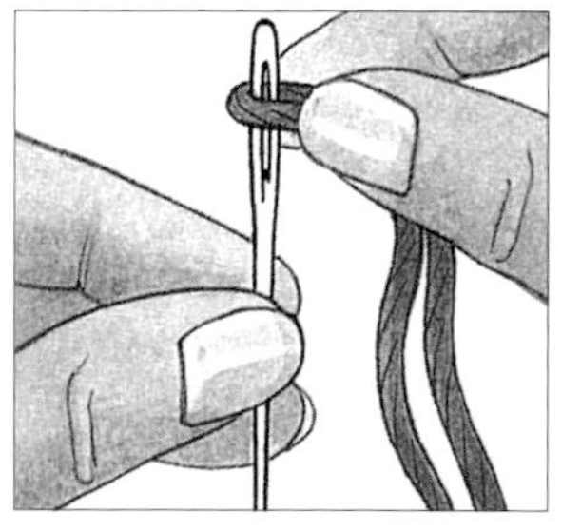

1 Double the thread a short distance from the end, then fold it around the needle eye.

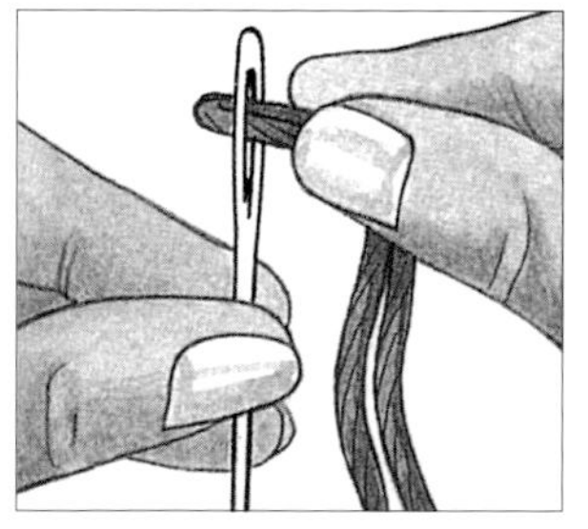

2 Push the folded thread through the needle eye as shown, holding the needle steady.

Using a Needle Threader

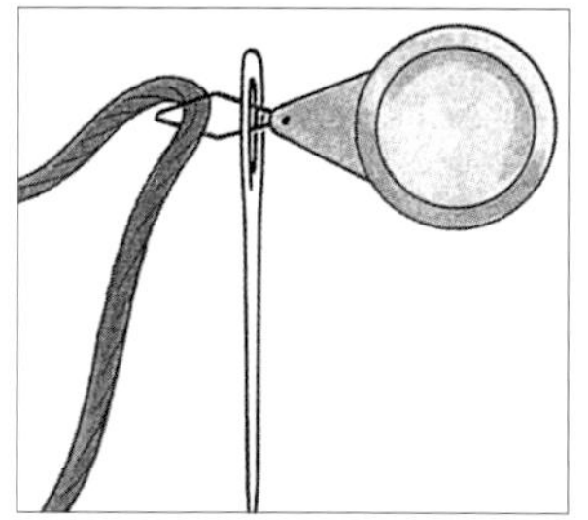

1 Push the wire loop through the needle eye; push the thread through the wire loop.

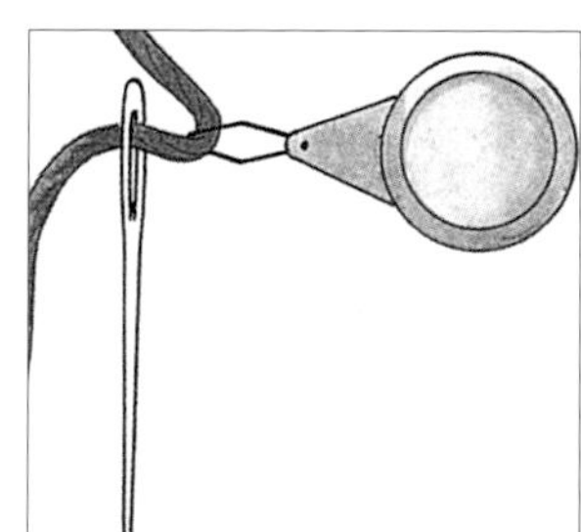

2 Carefully pull the wire loop with the inserted thread back through the needle eye.

Basic Stitch Techniques

Overstitching
Pull the threaded needle through the fabric, leaving a tail at the back 4 cm (1½ in) long. Begin stitching, securing the tail at the back by the stitches.

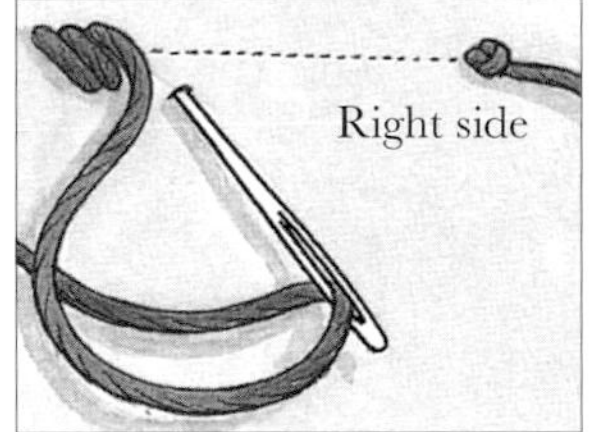

Using knots
Work left to right. Position knot 4 cm (1½ in) to right of first stitch on front. Work stitches over thread at back. When secure, cut off knot and pull tail to back.

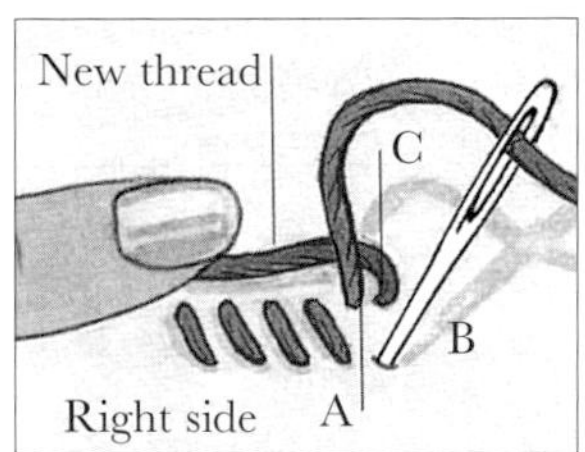

Changing threads mid-row
Come up at A. Thread a new needle and come up at C. Hold thread as shown, go down at B with old thread and fasten off.

Finishing off
Take needle and thread through to the back of fabric and weave in and out of three or four adjacent stitches. Gently pull the thread through.

Straight Stitch Family

Straight Stitch

Straight stitch is very simple and versatile. I use it in an irregular way for hair, grass, clusters of flower stems, leaves and tree branches.

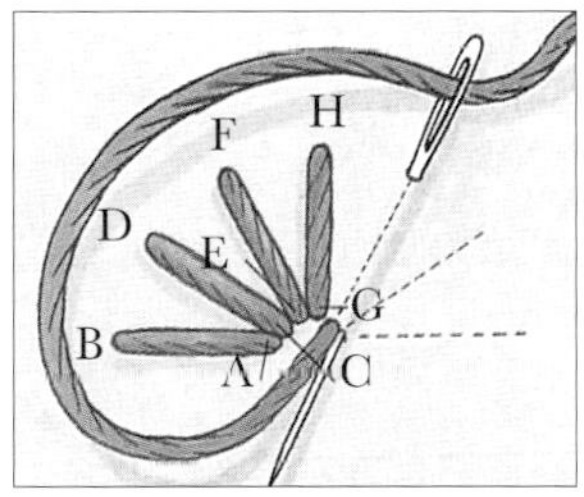

1 To create a straight-stitch fan, come up at A, go down at B, up at C. Repeat, going down at D, up at E, down at F, up at G, and down at H.

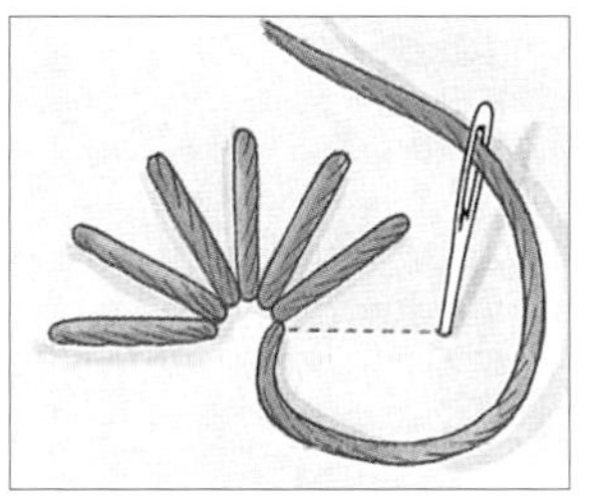

2 Continue working in this way until you have worked a half-circle of evenly spaced stitches. Tie off thread at the back of your work.

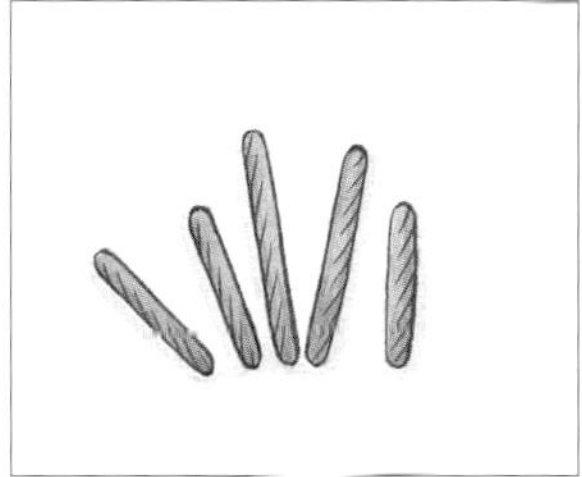

Irregular straight stitch
Work a detached stitch by repeating Step 1 in an irregular way. Pull through and anchor.

Running Stitch

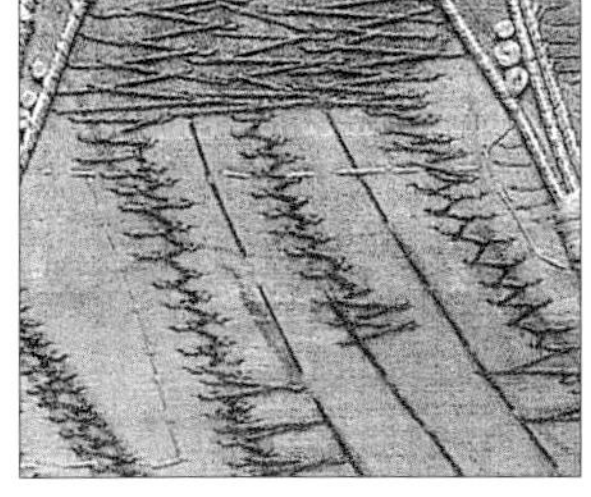

Used for outlining objects and forms, or for creating areas of texture in paths or stonework.

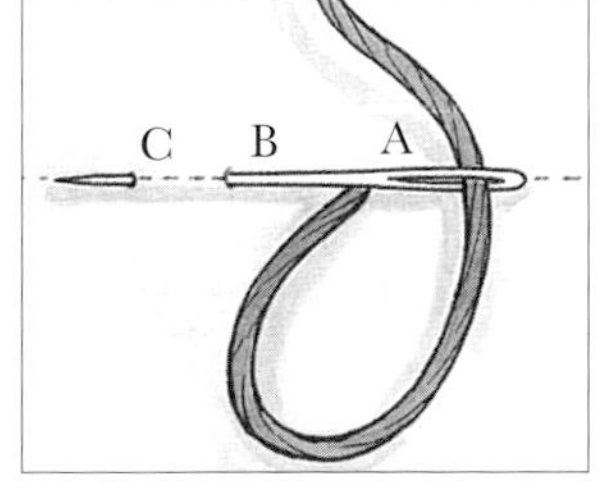

1 Come up at A, go down at B, then come up at C. Do not pull thread through fabric.

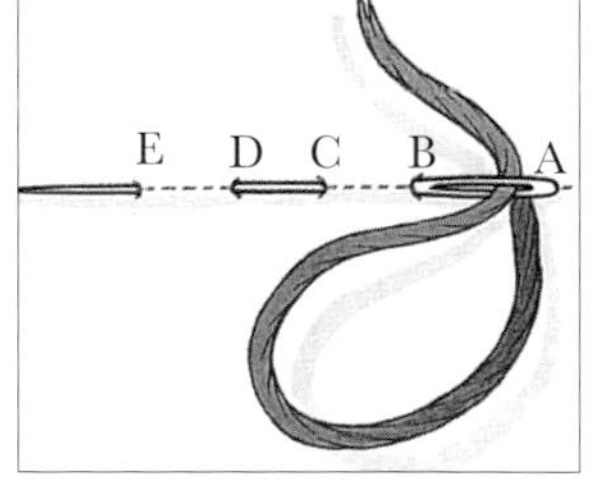

2 Go down at D, come up at E. Pull thread through gently, so fabric does not pucker.

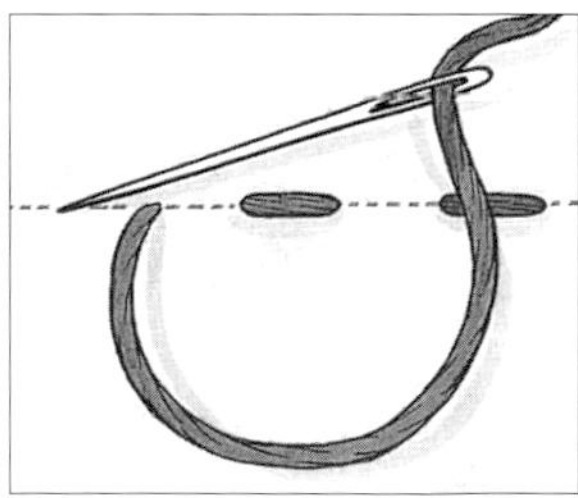

3 Continue following design line as shown, by repeating Steps 1 and 2.

Backstitch

A useful stitch for outlining shapes over a densely stitched background. Ideal for curved lines such as flower stems.

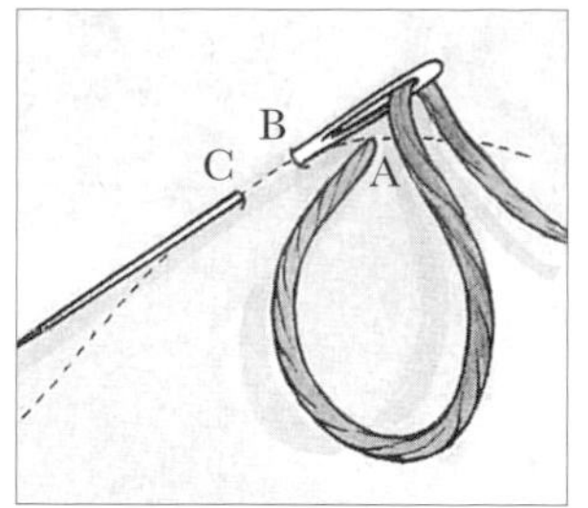

1 Working from right to left, come up at A, go down at B, then come up at C. Pull thread through.

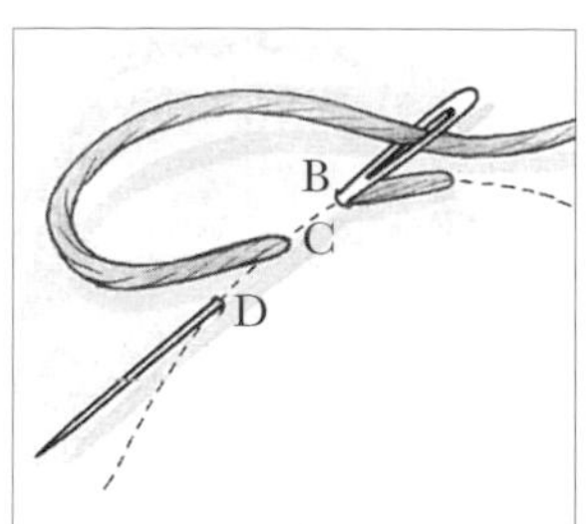

2 Go down again at B to make a backstitch, then come up at D, ready for the next stitch.

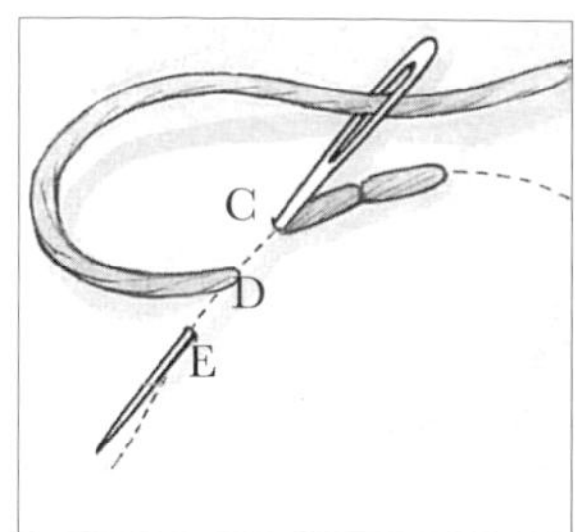

3 Pull thread through, then go down at C and come up at E. Repeat as above to work a backstitched line.

Satin Stitch

This is a filling stitch that creates a silky surface. Keep the tension even to avoid puckering.

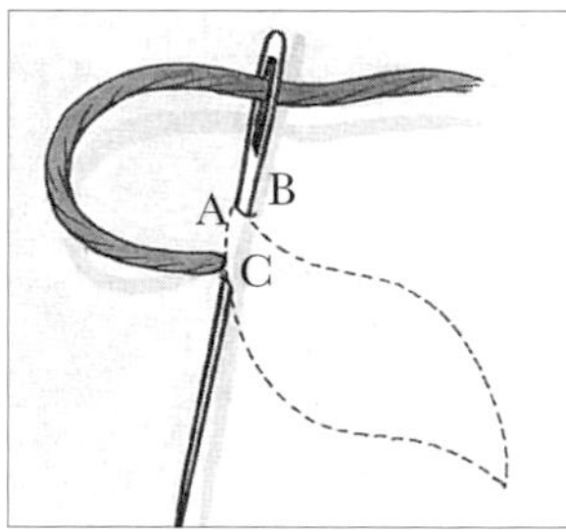

1 Come up at A, go down at B, and come up at C. Pull thread through gently, ready for the next stitch.

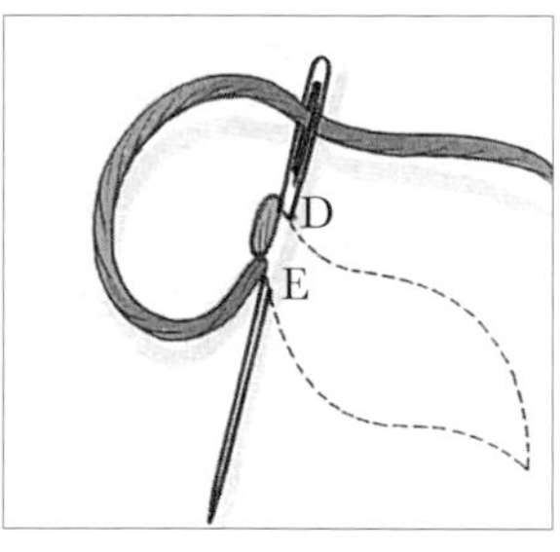

2 Placing stitches close together, go down at D and come up at E. Follow exact guidelines of motif to make even edge.

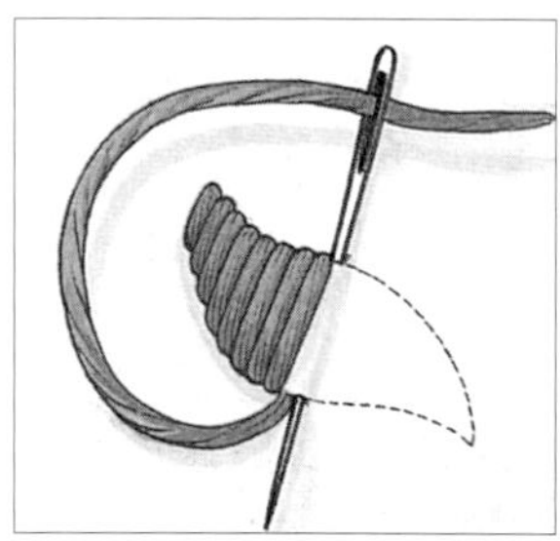

3 Continue to fill the motif in this manner, keeping an even tension so that the surface remains smooth.

Herringbone Stitch

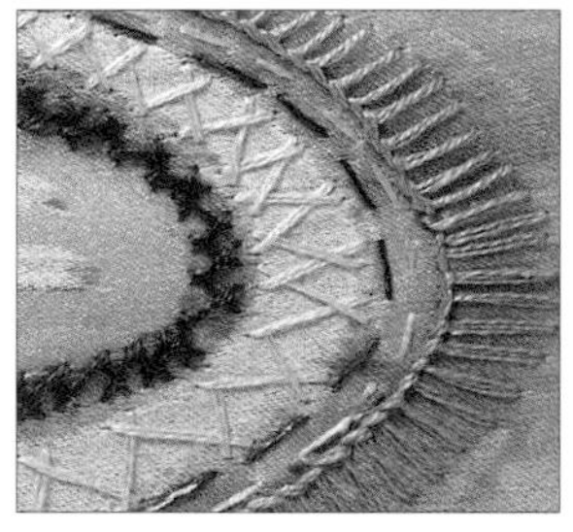

A decorative stitch that combines well with other simple stitches to create a pattern when used as part of an overall design.

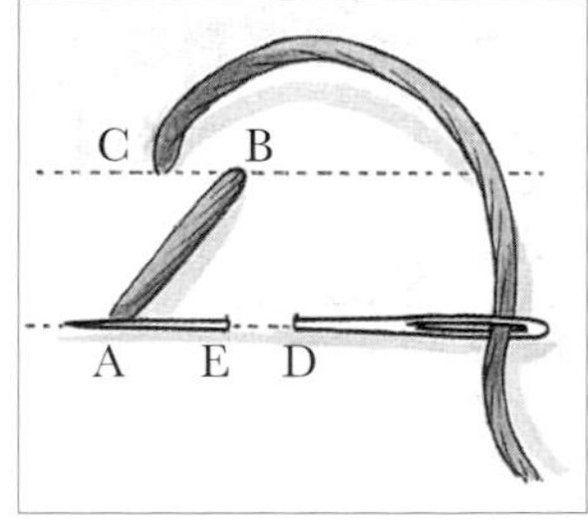

1 Come up at A, go down at B, come up at C. Cross down and insert at D, coming up at E. Threads will cross at top.

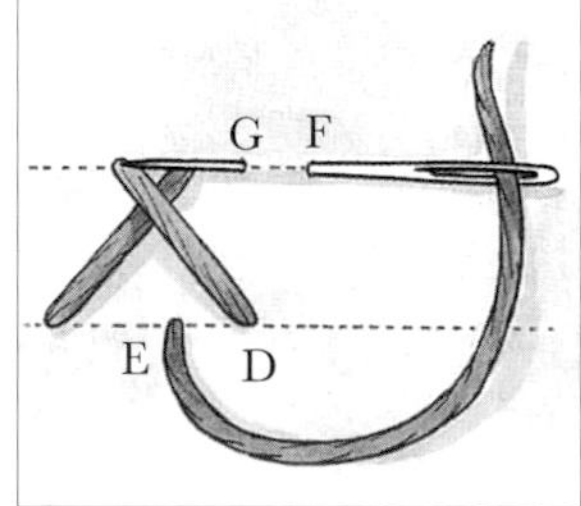

2 Cross up and insert at F, then come up at G. Pull through. Threads will cross at bottom.

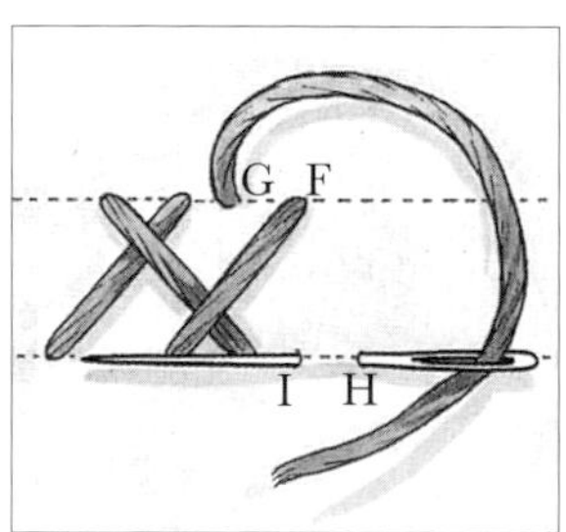

3 Cross down and insert at H, coming up at I. Continue along row by repeating Steps 1 and 2.

Seed Stitch

This is a random filling stitch that creates a textured surface. It is particularly good for depicting paths and patches of ground, and for decorating surfaces.

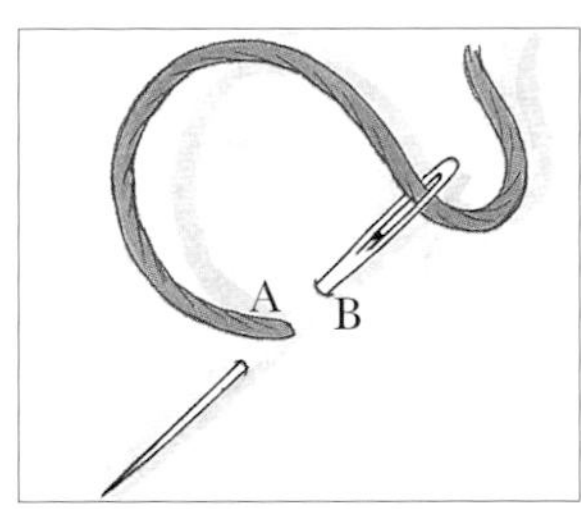

1 Come up at A and go down at B. Come up again where you want the next stitch to start.

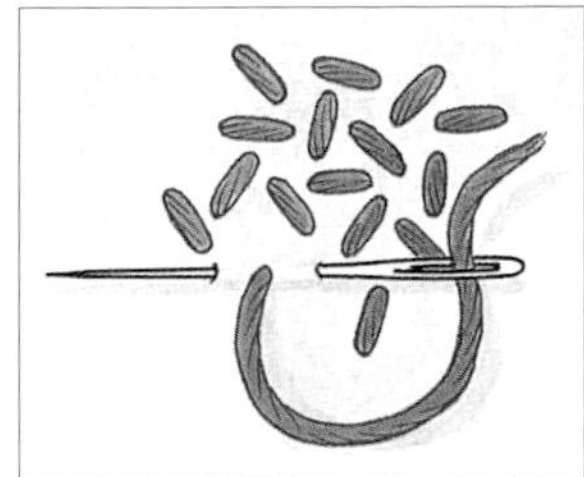

2 Work small stitches at random angles, to fill in the design shape or background area.

Stem Stitch

One of the best-known outline stitches, it can also be used to make grass, stems and branches.

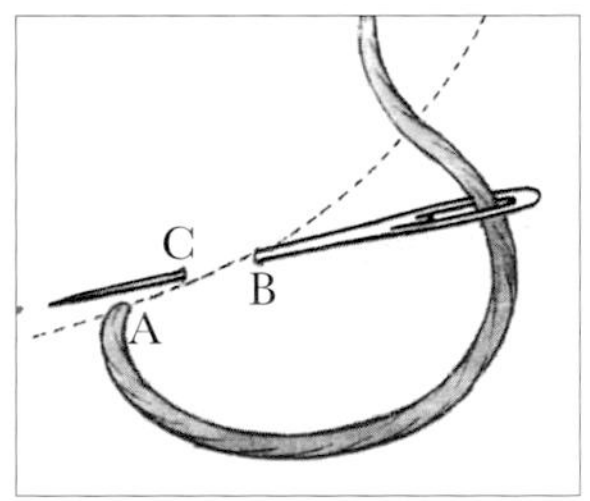

1 Come up at A, go down at B, come up at C above working thread. Pull thread through.

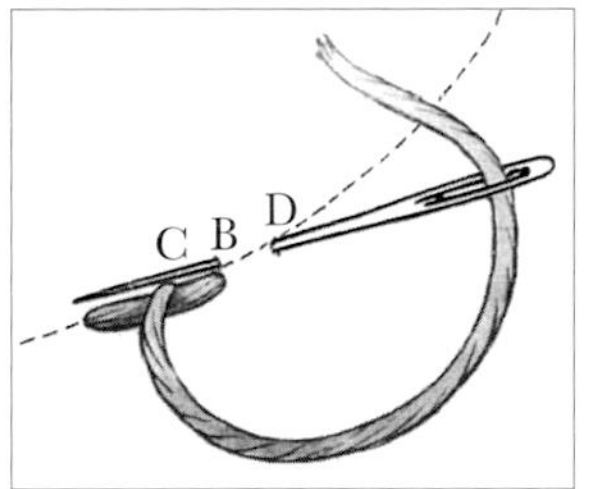

2 Keeping the working thread under the needle, go down at D and come up at B to complete the second stitch.

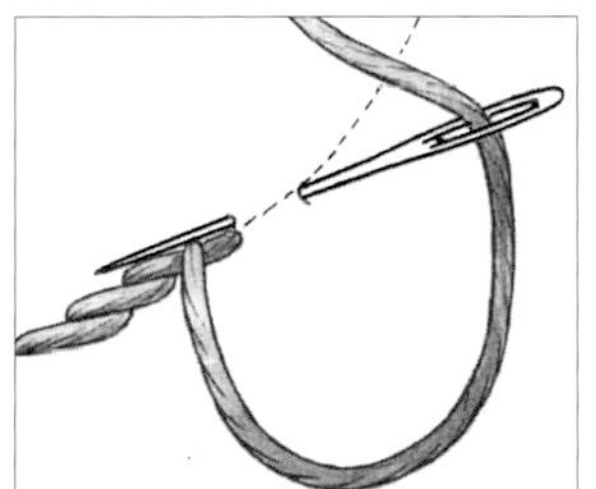

3 Repeat Step 2 to continue stitching along row as shown, keeping the stitches evenly sized.

Leaf Stitch

A filling stitch that creates especially effective leaves and flowers. Here it is inverted to create petals and flower heads.

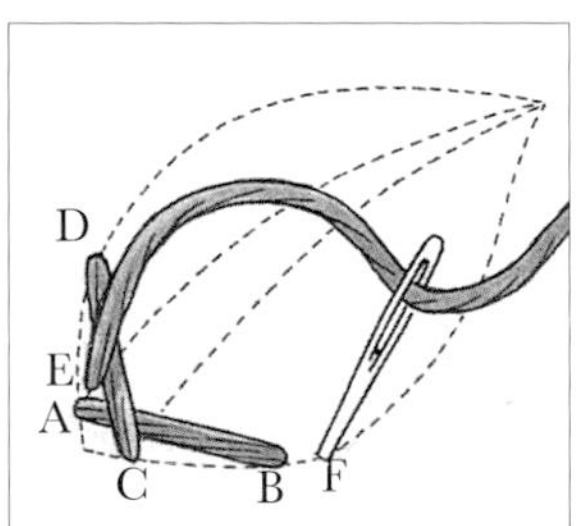

1 Come up at A, go down at B, and come up at C. Go down at D to form central cross, and come up at E, directly in line with A. Go down at F, just next to B.

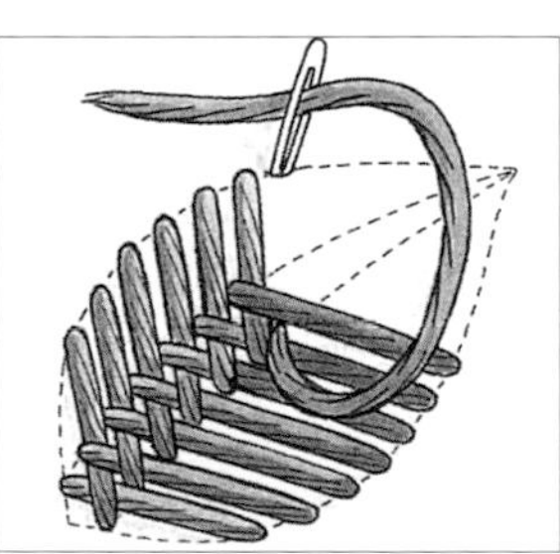

2 Continue in this way to form a bank of stitches crossed in the centre. Graduate stitch length, and be sure that the spaces between each stitch are even.

Padded Satin Stitch

Basically a double satin stitch worked in two layers in opposite directions, it is used to make thick, three-dimensional areas.

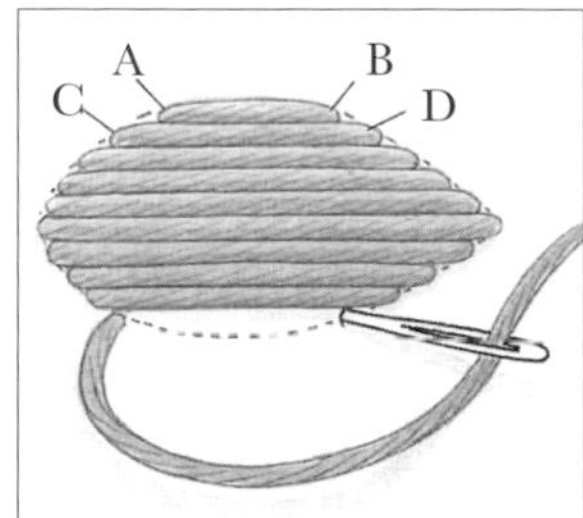

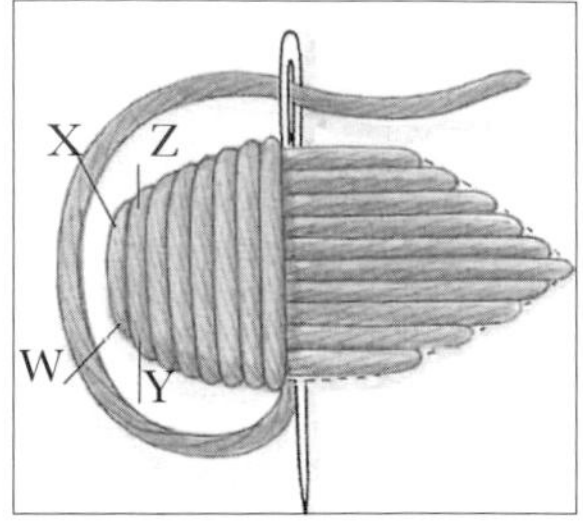

1 Come up at A, go down at B, up at C, and down at D. Continue to fill the motif with basic satin stitch. Secure the thread.

2 Come up at W, go down at X, up at Y, and down at Z. Continue until base stitches are completely covered.

Eyelet Stitch

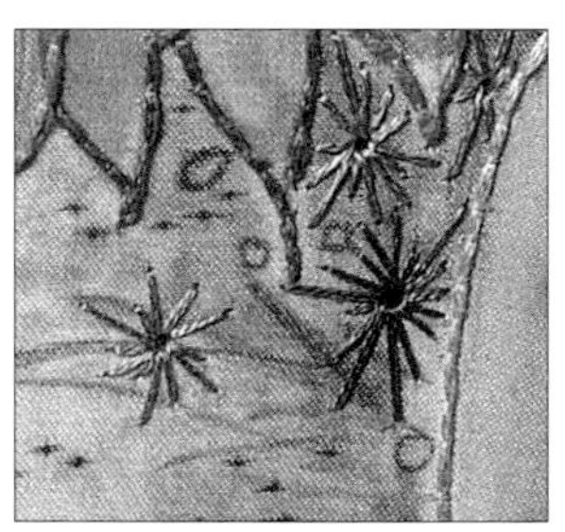

Effective for suggesting flower heads. I have used it as a background filling stitch in the sunflower painting.

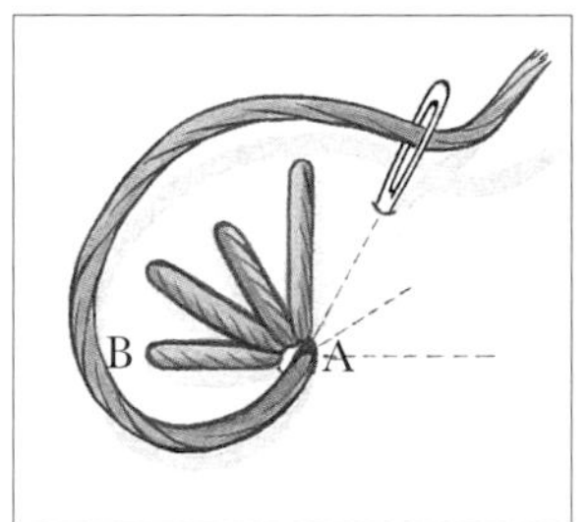

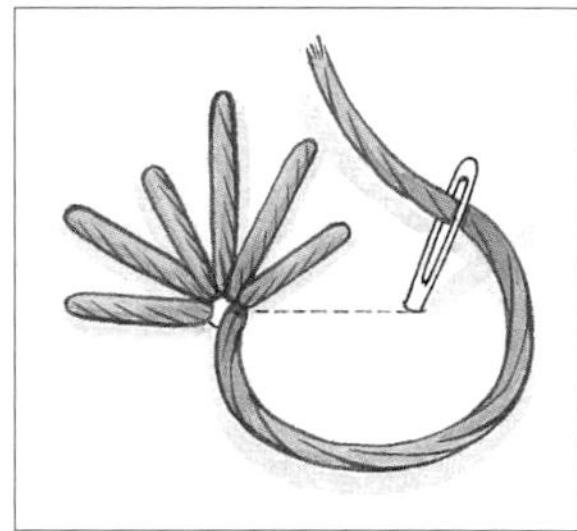

1 Come up at A and go down at B. Come up again in the same hole each time and repeat.

2 Work stitches of varying lengths, always working from the same central hole.

3 Work stitches at random angles, to fill in a design shape or background area.

Knotted Stitch Family

Bullion Knot

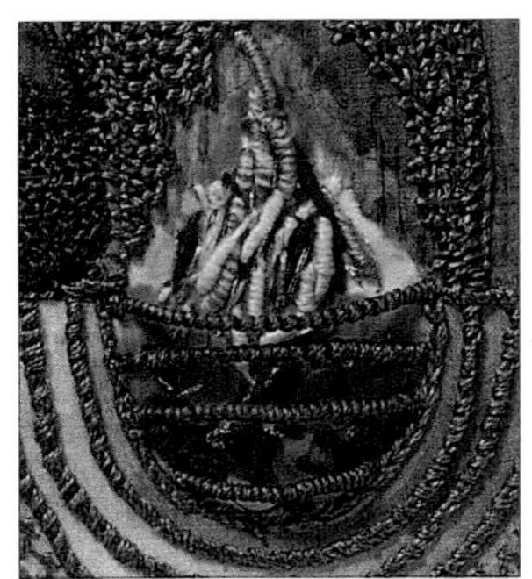

An elongated knot that is useful for making flowers, especially roses and peonies, and for decorating all manner of objects, such as the flames in this picture.

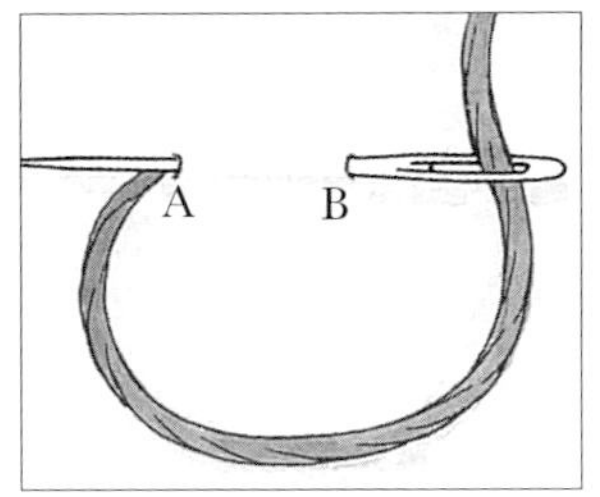

1 Come up at A, go down at B, and back up at A, as though forming backstitch. Do not pull needle through.

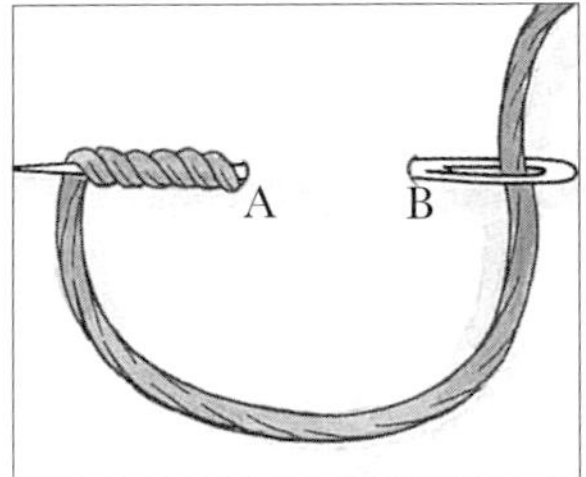

2 Wind thread around needle point until a length equal to or greater than the distance between A and B is covered.

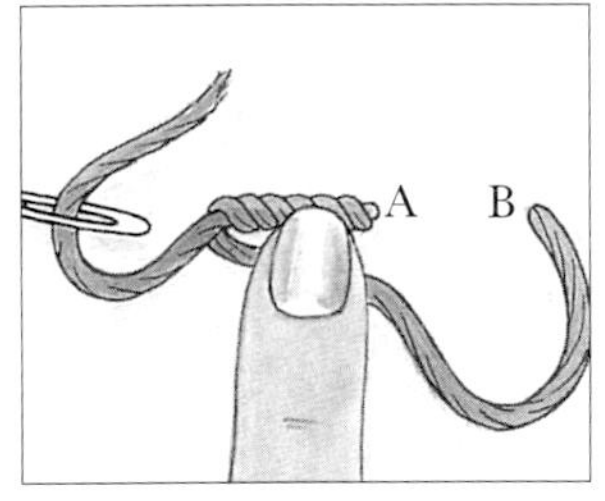

3 Hold down coiled threads with finger and pull needle through gently. Be careful not to distort coil by pulling the thread too hard.

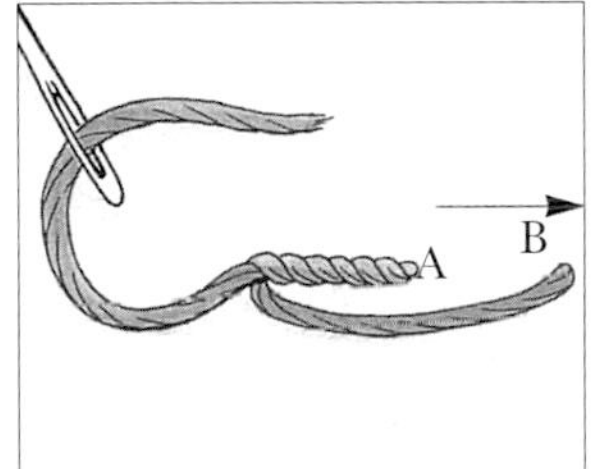

4 Stitch now resembles a coiled cord. Bring needle to right to move coil in place between A and B. Pull extra thread through to take up slack.

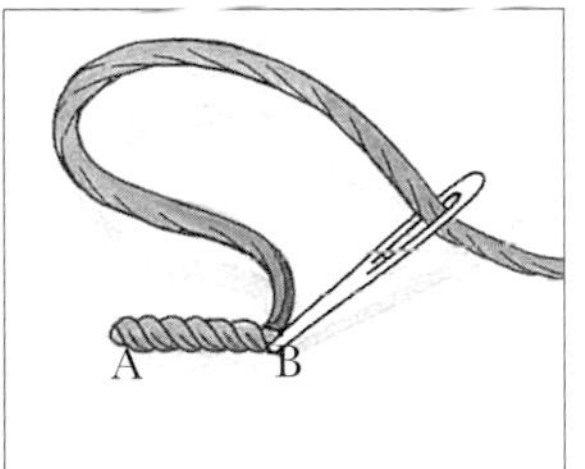

5 Go down at B again to anchor stitch in place. If coil is longer than A–B, coil will roll up on the fabric surface, giving three-dimensional effect.

French Knot

These tiny knotted stitches make effective flowers, and also work well for depicting curly hair. Can be used as a filling stitch.

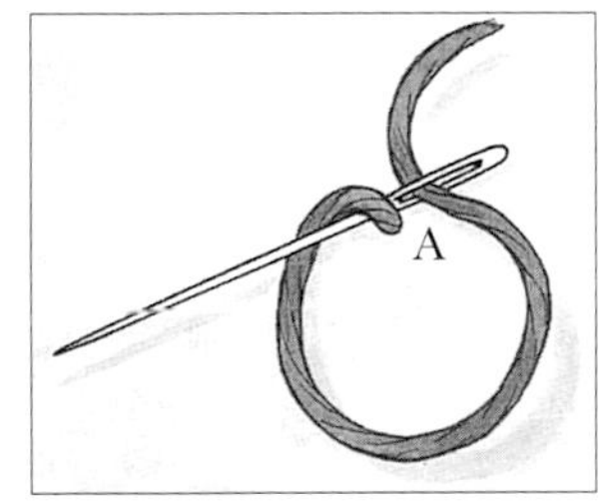

1 Come up at A, and wrap thread around needle once in counter-clockwise direction.

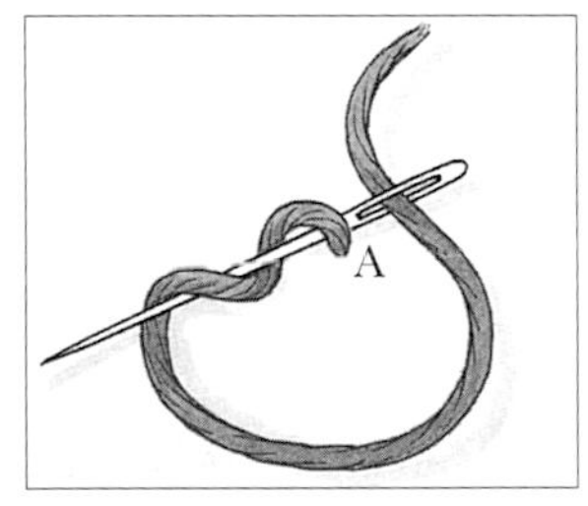

2 Wrap thread around needle a second time in same direction, keeping needle away from fabric.

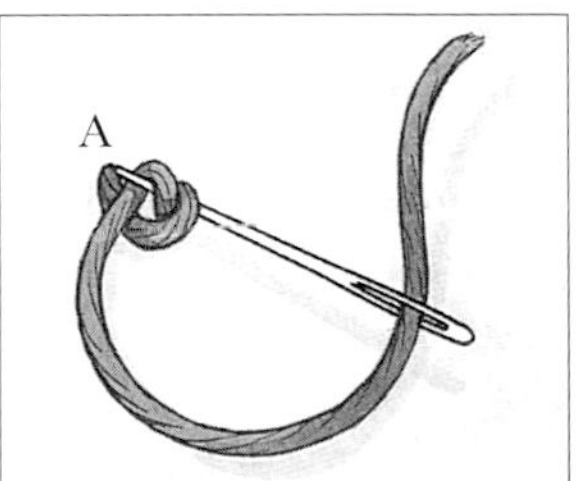

3 Push wraps together and slide to end of needle. Go back down close to the starting point, pulling needle and thread through to form knot.

Looped Stitch Family

Cretan Stitch

One of the most versatile of all looped stitches, it can be used to make clouds, water, grass, fields, clothing and animal fur. I use an irregular Cretan stitch that is approximately 10–12 cm (4–5 in) in length.

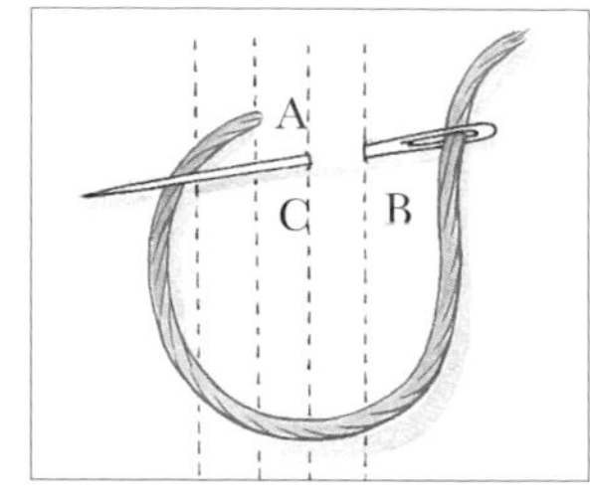

1 Come up at A, go down at B, and up at C, keeping the work ing thread under the needle point.

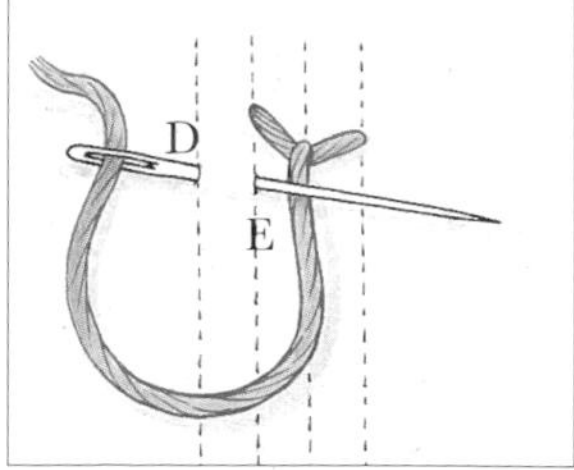

2 Go down at D (at a random point or following a motif outline) and come up at E, keeping the thread under the needle point.

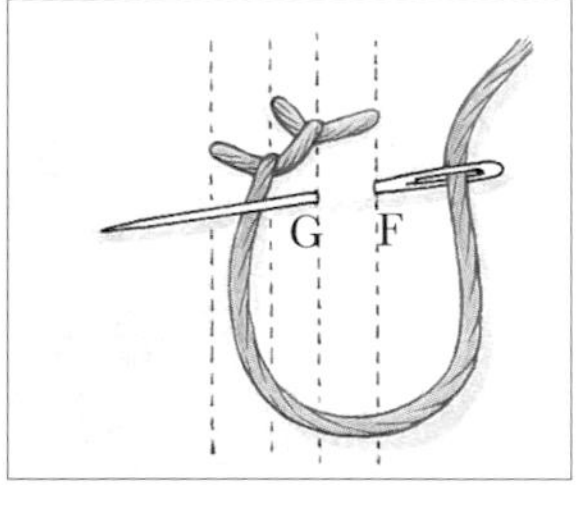

3 Go down at F and up at G, as before. Work at random or follow guidelines.

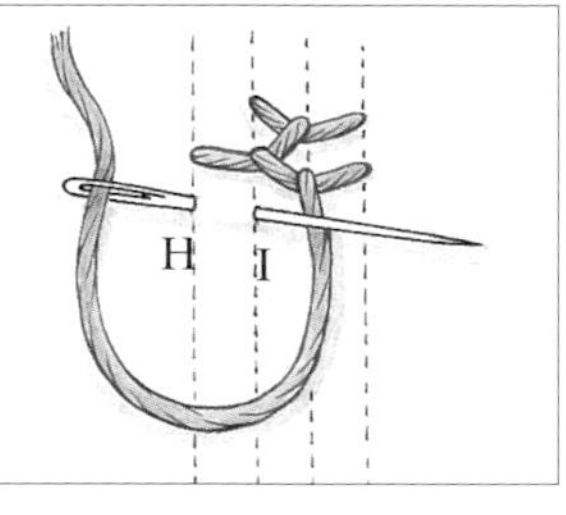

4 Go down at H and up at I and continue in the same fashion.

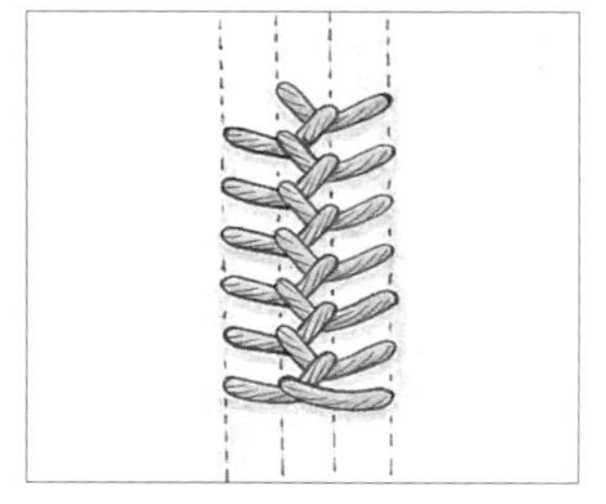

5 Continue working stitches as before, always keeping the working thread under the needle point.

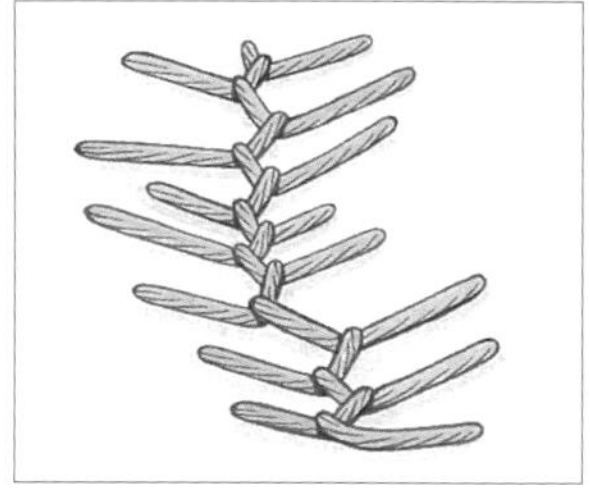

Irregular Cretan stitch
Working stitches of different lengths and widths creates an irregular line of filling that can be worked over again for more texture.

Open Buttonhole Stitch (Blanket Stitch)

Used in place of close-worked buttonhole stitch for a more open effect.

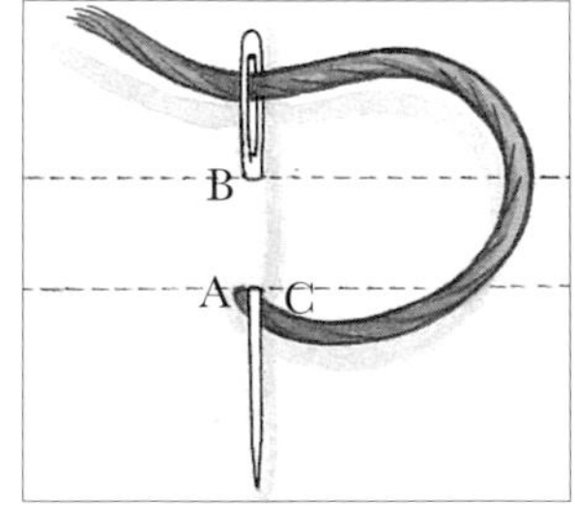

1 Come up at A, go down at B, come up at C, just to immediate right of A. Carry thread under needle point from left to right.

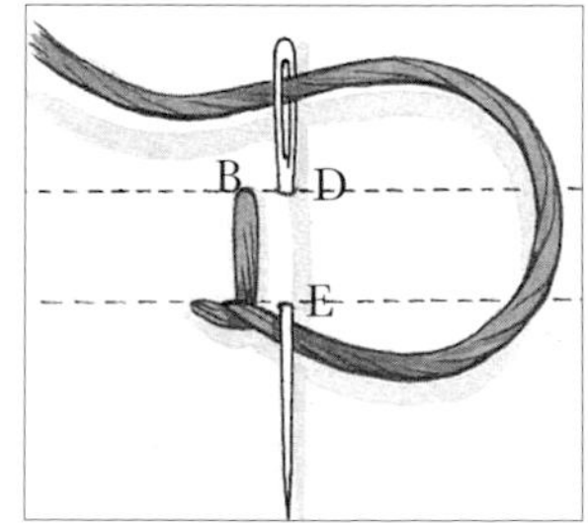

2 Go down at D (a short space to the right of B). Come up at E, keeping thread under needle point.

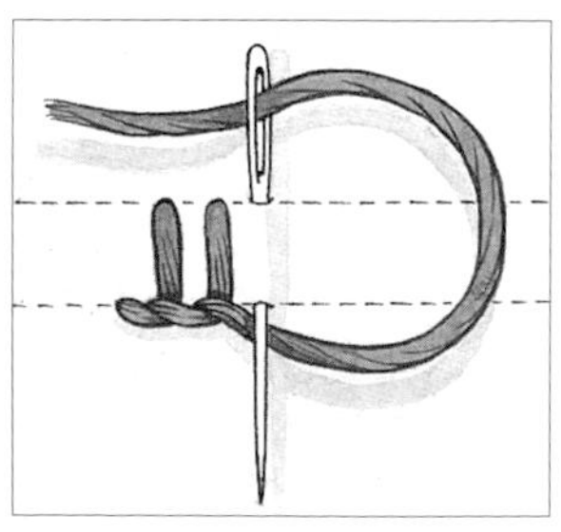

3 Continue in this way along the row, keeping all stitches evenly spaced.

Buttonhole Stitch

It can be worked in a circle or in straight or curved lines. It is useful for making decorations on all manner of items.

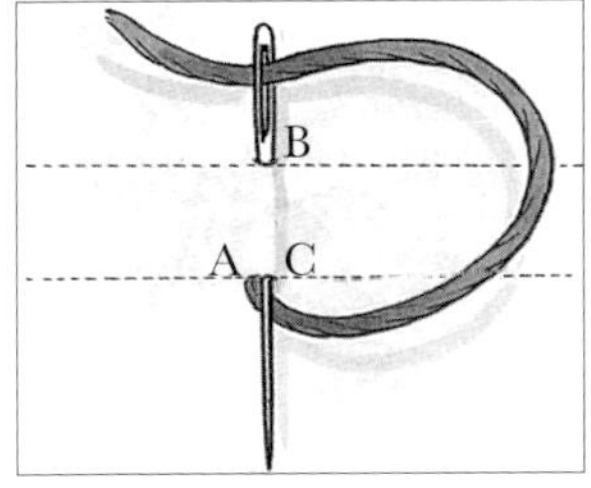

1 Come up at A, go down at B, come up at C, just to immediate right of A. Carry thread under needle point from left to right. Pull thread through.

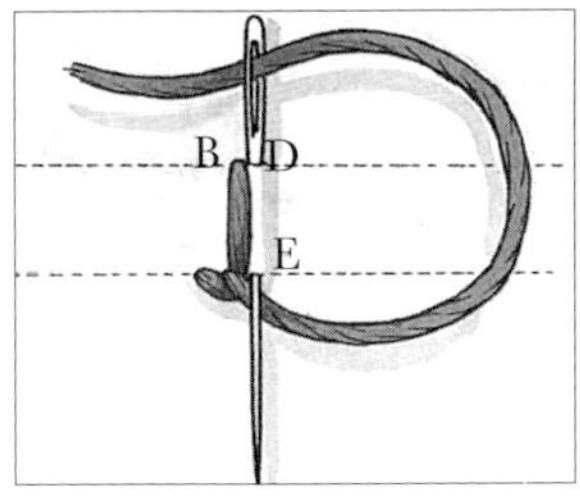

2 Go down at D (just to immediate right of B). Come up at E, keeping the thread under the needle point.

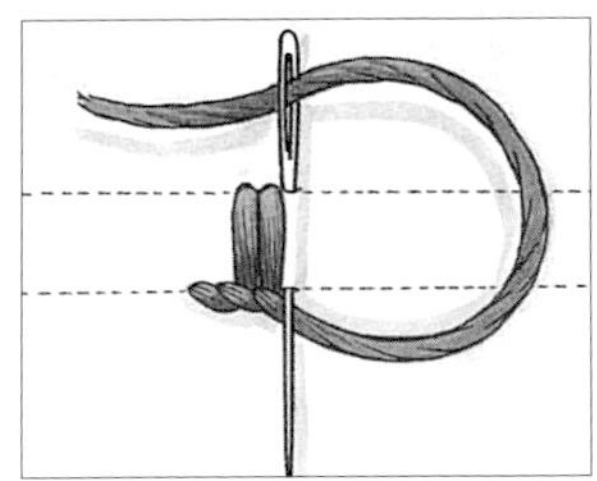

3 Continue in this way along the row, keeping all stitches even and close together as shown.

Buttonhole Filling Stitch

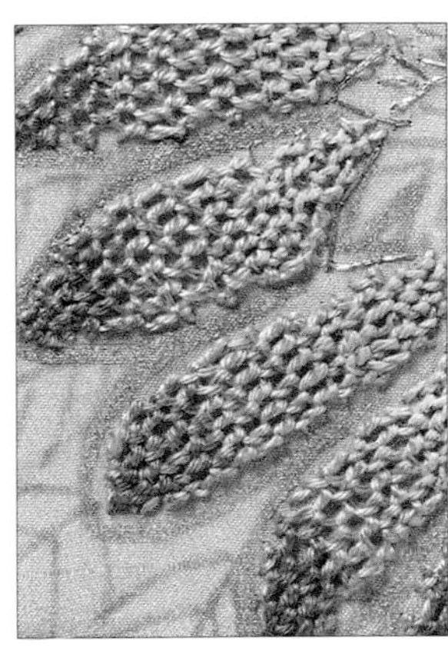

Useful for making lacy clothing and textiles. Each row is worked through the background fabric to create a firm, stable needlelace texture. The first row is worked in a similar way to buttonhole stitch above. The stitch can be worked in single or double stitches.

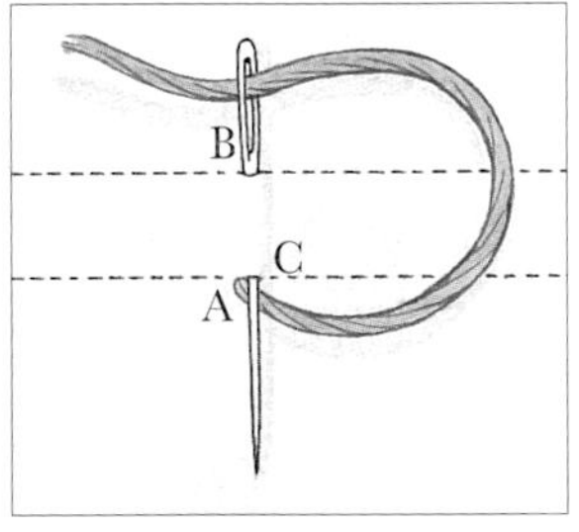

1 Come up at A, go down at B and up again at C, just next to A, keeping the working thread under the point of the needle.

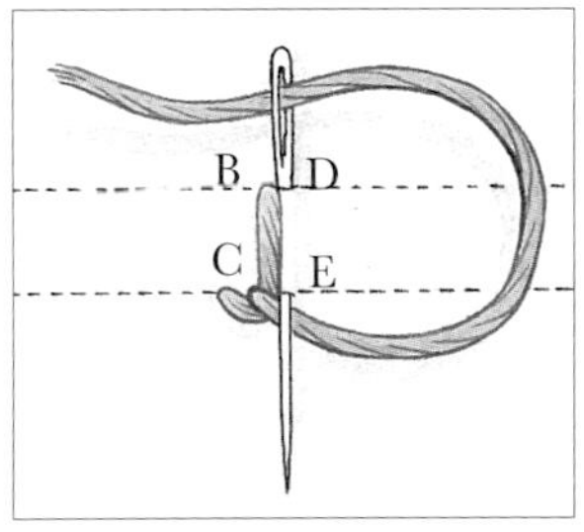

2 Pull thread through and go down at D, immediately to the right of B. Go down at E, just next to C, with the thread under the needle point. Pull thread through.

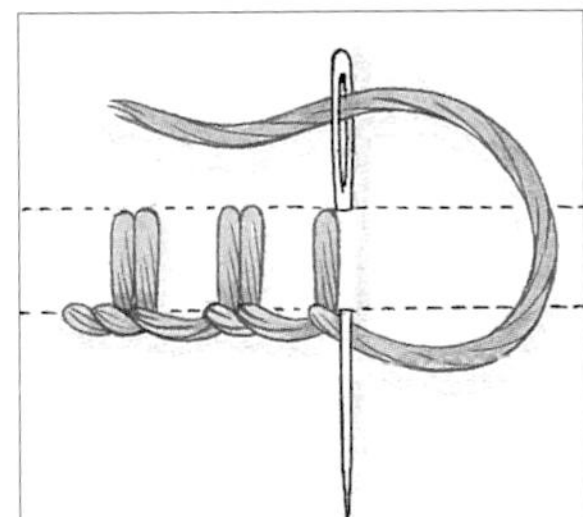

3 Make pairs of upright stitches along the entire length of the guidelines.

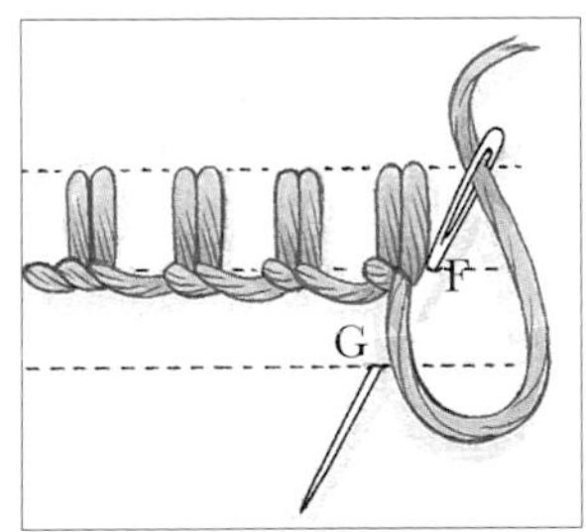

4 At the end of the row finish with a stitch at F, just next to the final loop, and come up at G to start the next row.

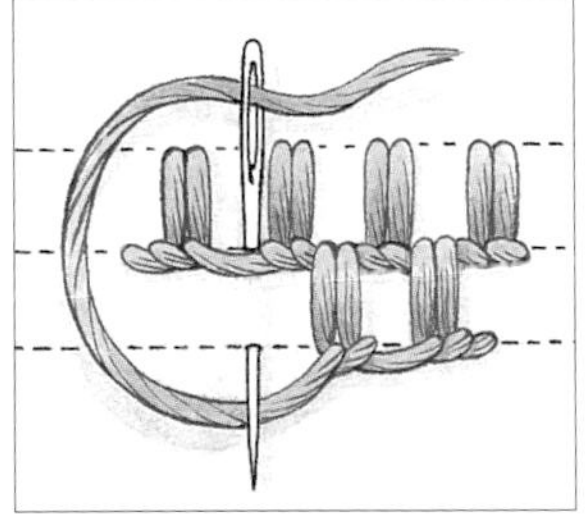

5 Work pairs of stitches as before but in the opposite direction. Take the thread through the loops in the previous row and out through the fabric.

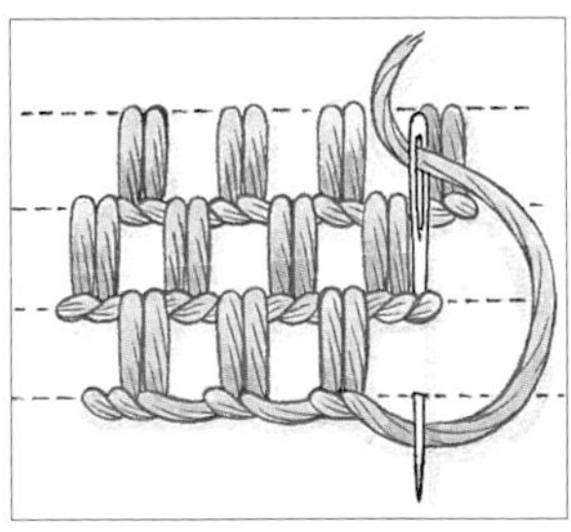

6 Continue in this way, working rows in alternate directions, until the area is filled.

Detached Buttonhole Stitch

Another needlelace stitch, which creates a firm, opaque fabric. It is based on buttonhole stitch, but the rows of stitching are not worked through the background fabric, so the bottom edge is not attached to the background, making it especially effective for creating garments.

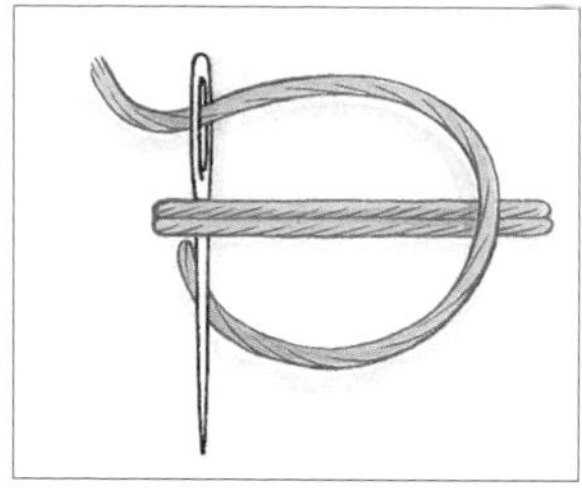

1 Lay two threads across the top of the entire width to be covered. Without taking the needle through the background fabric, make a buttonhole stitch over the left-hand end of the laid threads.

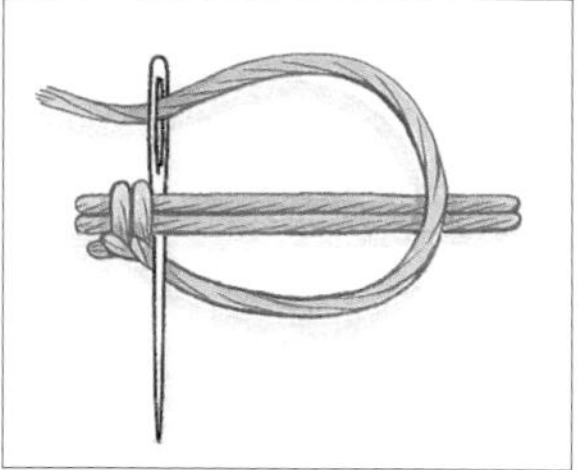

2 Always keeping the working thread under the needle point, cover the line of laid threads with buttonhole stitches.

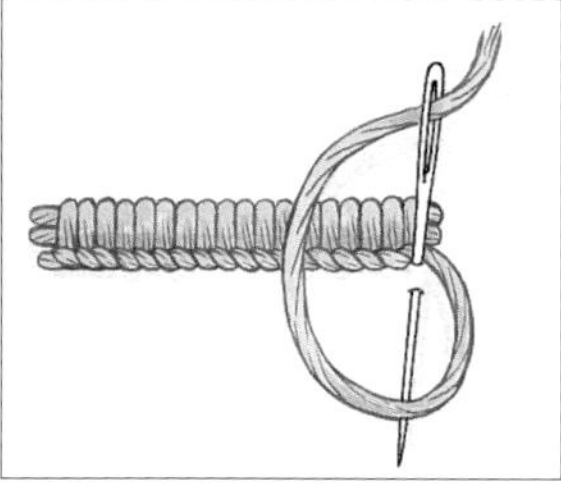

3 At the end of the row, keep the thread under the needle point, take the needle through background fabric directly beneath the end of the laid threads.

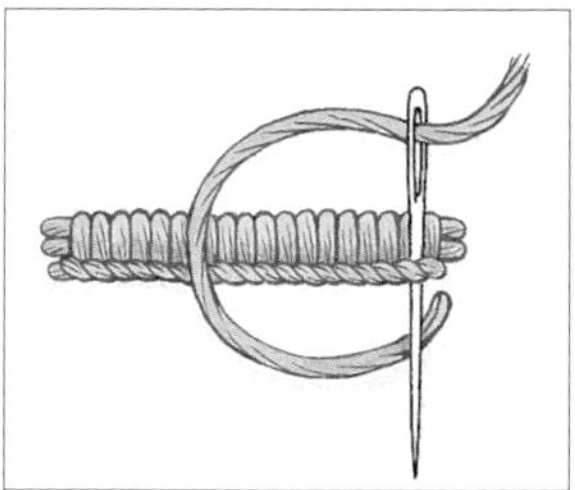

4 Take the needle through the first loop at the bottom of the row above to make an un anchored buttonhole stitch.

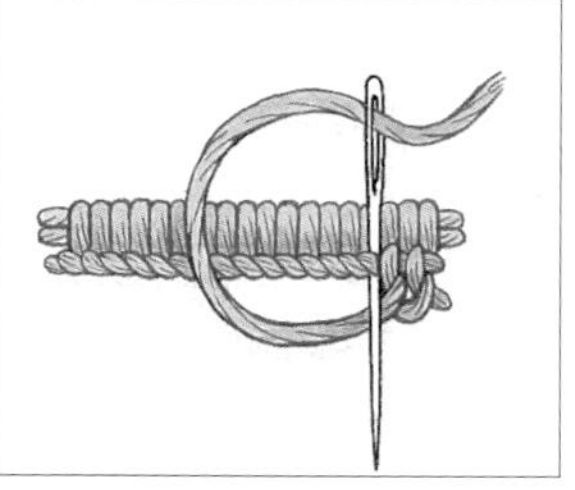

5 Work in the opposite direction to make a row of buttonhole stitches that do not go through the background fabric.

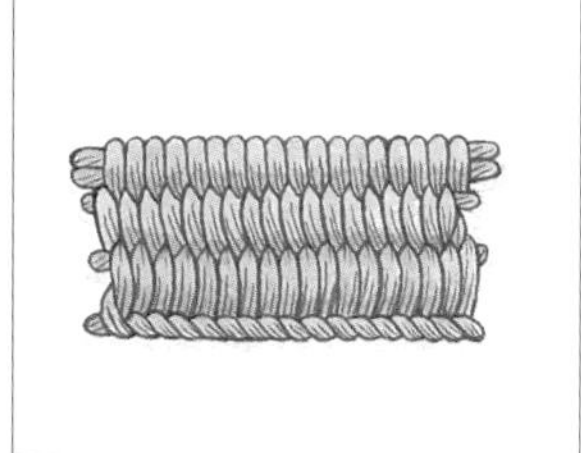

6 Repeat Step 3 at the end of each row and work back in the opposite direction until the area is covered.

Closed Buttonhole Stitch

This buttonhole stitch is worked in a triangular shape. Closed buttonhole is especially useful for outlining and decorating all kinds of objects.

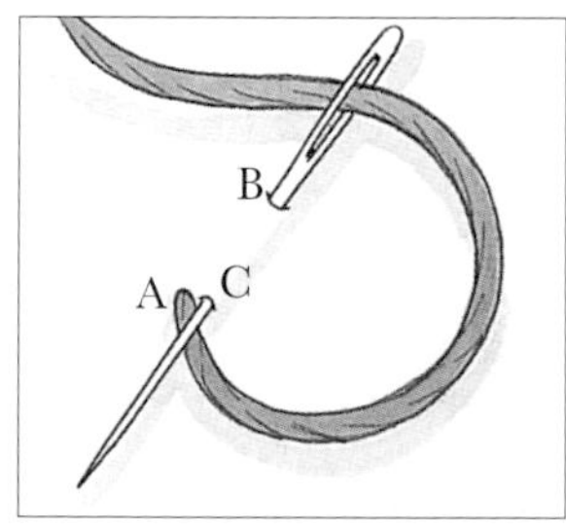

1 Come up at A, then go down at B and up at C as shown, keeping the needle under the working thread. Pull the thread through.

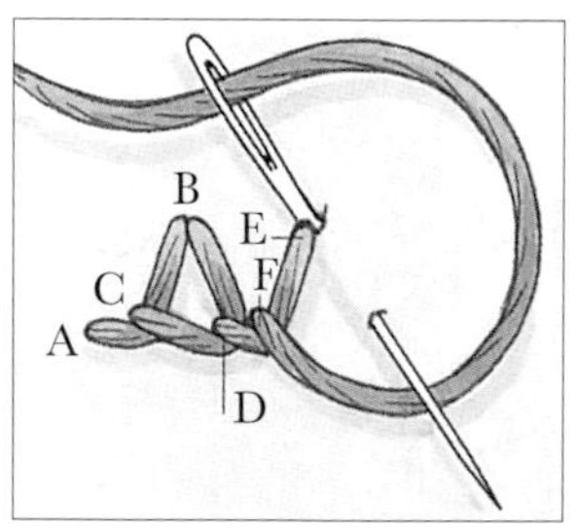

2 Go down next to B; come up at D with needle over working thread. Pull through. Go down at E, up at F, down next to E. Repeat from B in Step 1.

Treble Brussels Stitch

A needlelace stitch used to make clothing and lacy household textiles. Tension is crucial, because after the first row, only the ends of the rows are anchored through the background fabric.

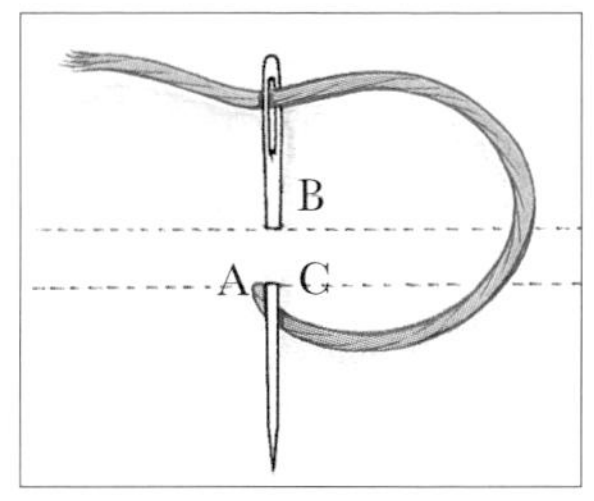

1 Come up at A, go down at B, and up at C, just next to A, keeping the working thread under the point of the needle.

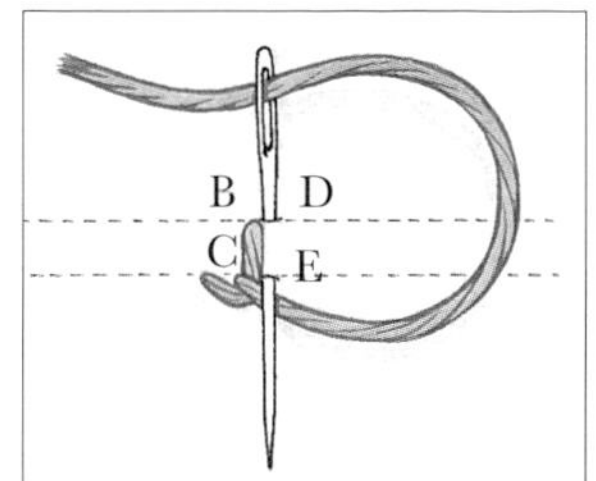

2 Pull the thread through and go down at D, immediately to the right of B. Come up at E, just next to C, and keep the thread under the needle point.

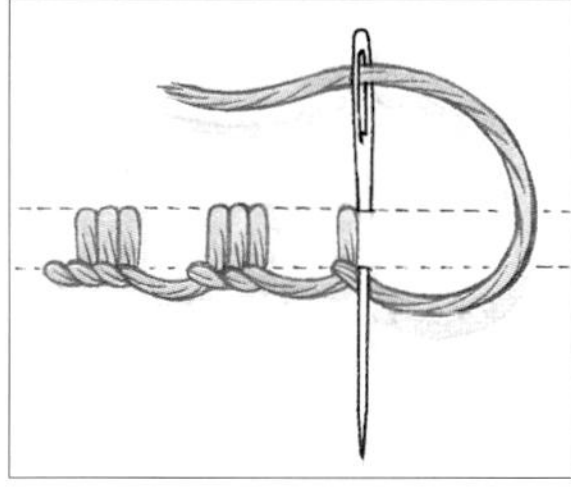

3 Work along the guidelines, making sets of three stitches with a loop between. Keep the spacing and the tension even.

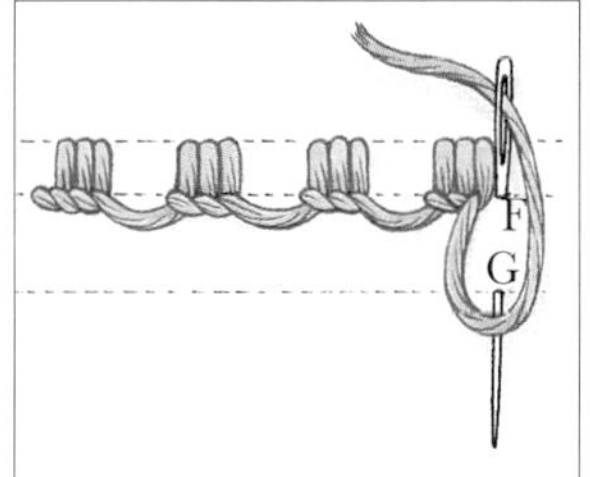

4 At the end of the first row, make a stitch at F just to the right of the final stitch. Come up at G to begin the next row with working thread under needle point.

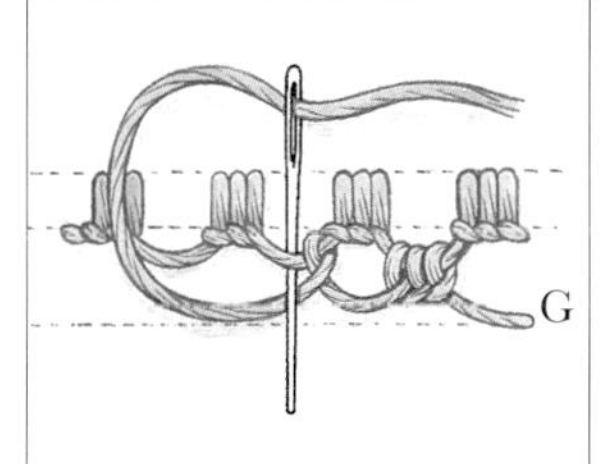

5 Taking the thread from G, make three buttonhole stitches into the first loop of the row above, working in the opposite direction.

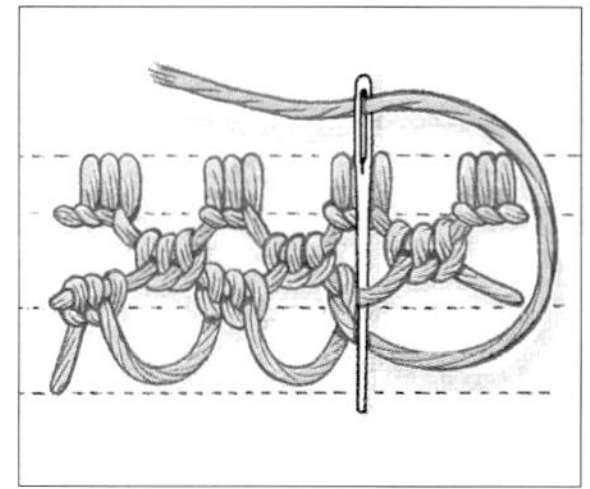

6 Continue working sets of three stitches into each loop of the previous row until the area has been filled.

Chain Stitch

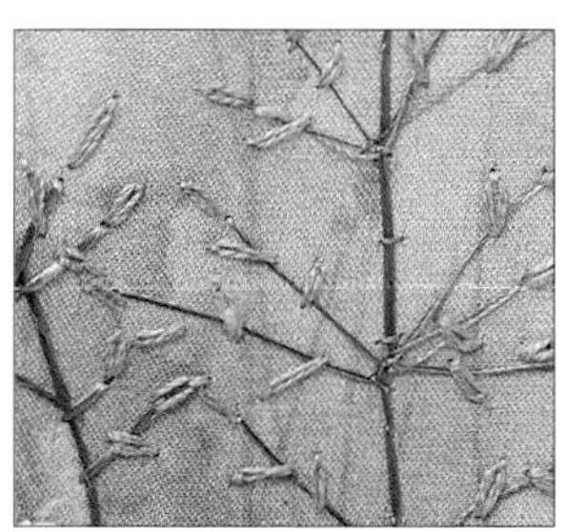

Its many uses include outlining and decorating objects, and making leaves, flowers, hair and eyes.

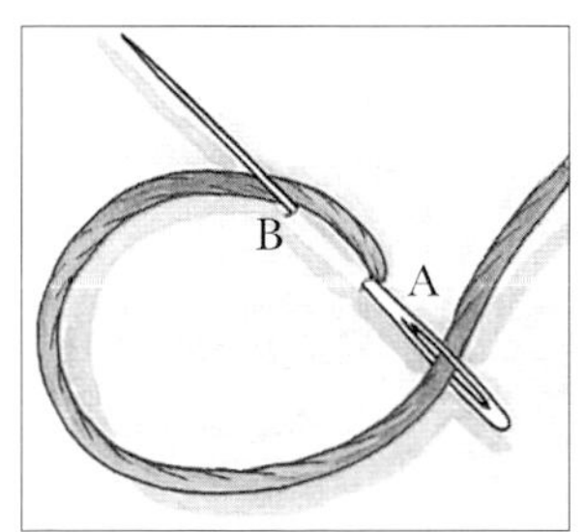

1 Come up at A. Go down to left of A, coming up at B. Loop thread under needle point from right to left.

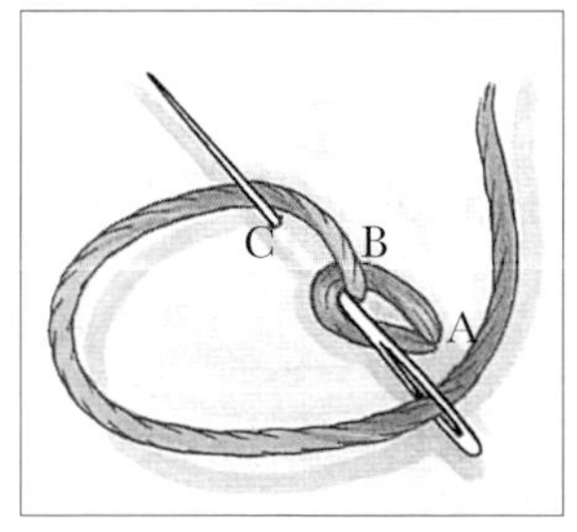

2 Pull thread through. Go down to left of B, inserting through loop, and come up at C. Loop thread as in Step 1.

Detached chain stitch
Work a detached stitch as in Step 1. Pull through and make a small stitch to anchor loop. A few detached stitches in a circle create a flower shape.

Zigzag Chain Stitch

Creates effective leaves and flowers when used over long thin stems of couched thread. Also useful for decorating and outlining objects or making grass along the edge of a path.

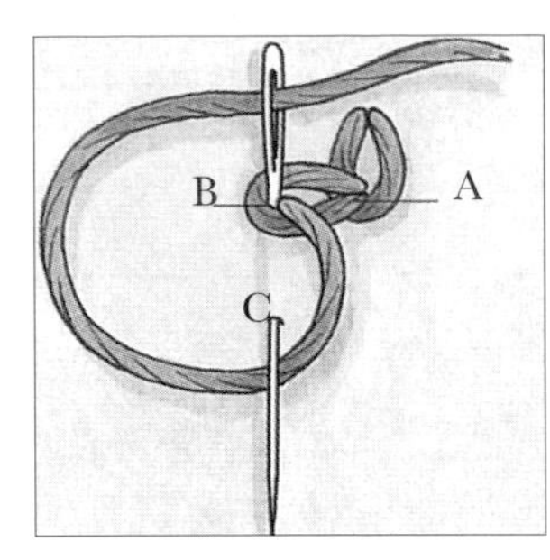

1 Come up at A inside first loop. Make second chain loop at an angle; go down next to A. Come up at B, go down next to B, and come up at C.

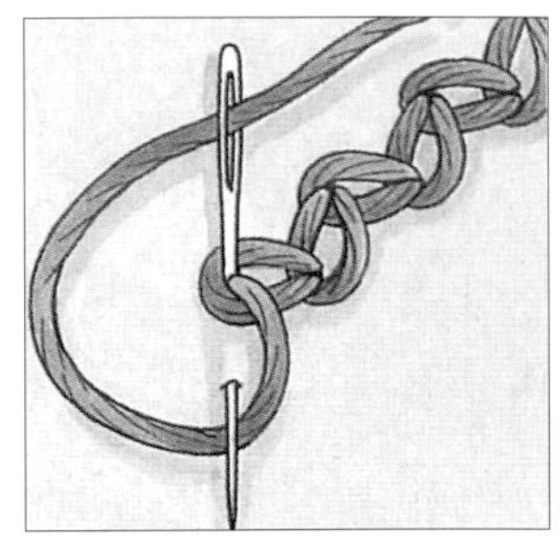

2 Continue to work the stitch, linking each chain loop as shown and alternating angle of loops to create a regular zigzag effect.

Looped Ring Picot

An edging stitch that creates texture and special effects on straight or curved lines. It is worked on a base row of buttonhole stitches. Keep the ring base thread fairly taut, as the covering stitches will pull it down.

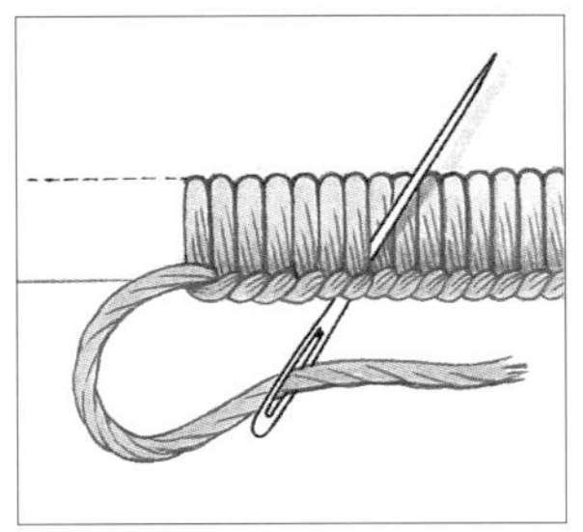

1 Make a row of buttonhole stitches. Take the needle through a loop some way from the end of the row, depending on how big you want the loops to be.

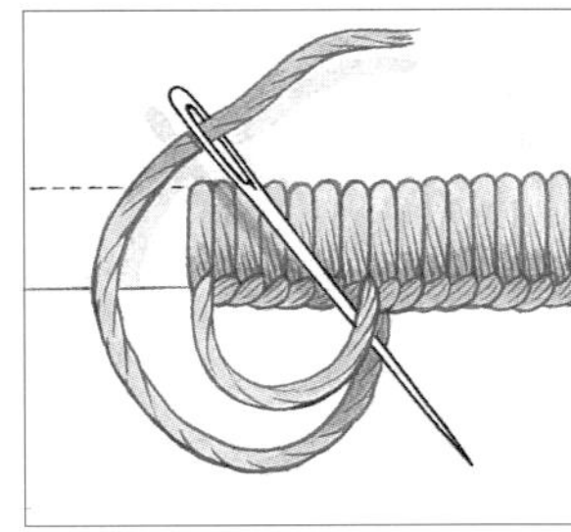

2 Make a buttonhole stitch at the point where the ring loop joins the base row.

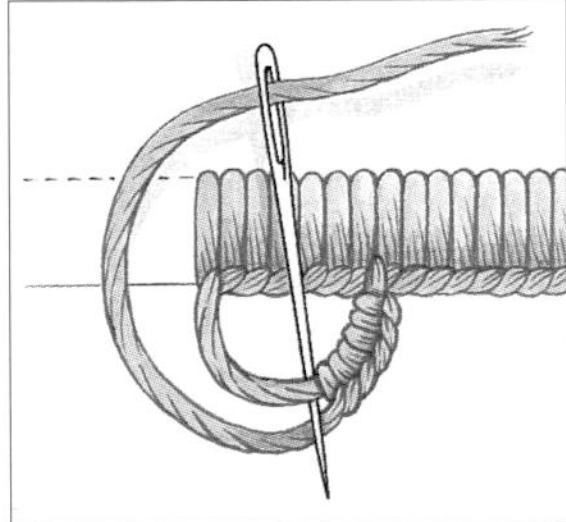

3 Cover the ring loop with buttonhole stitches to make the ring picot.

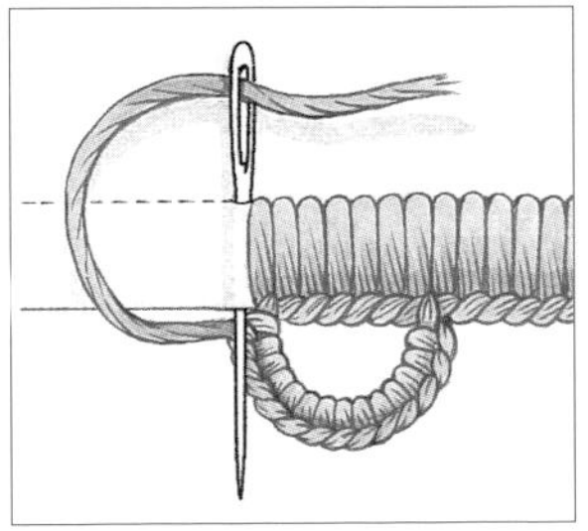

4 To continue the picot lace, carry on making base buttonhole stitches to the point where you want the next ring picot to be positioned.

Fly Stitch

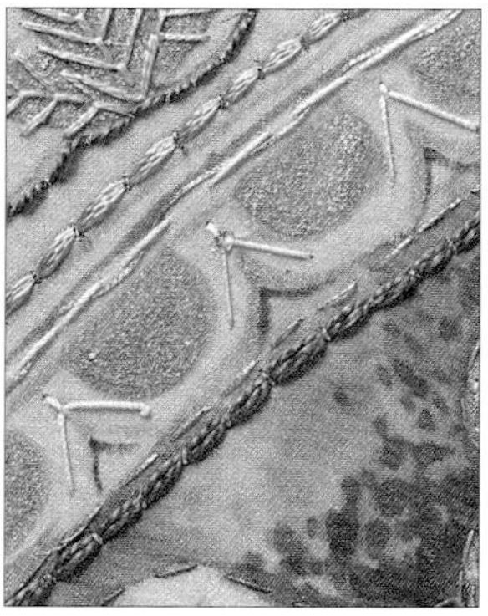

Fly stitch can be used to create flowers, hair and leaves, and for texturing background areas. It is very versatile and the look can be altered completely by changing the size of each part of the stitch and the angle of the tie-down stitch.

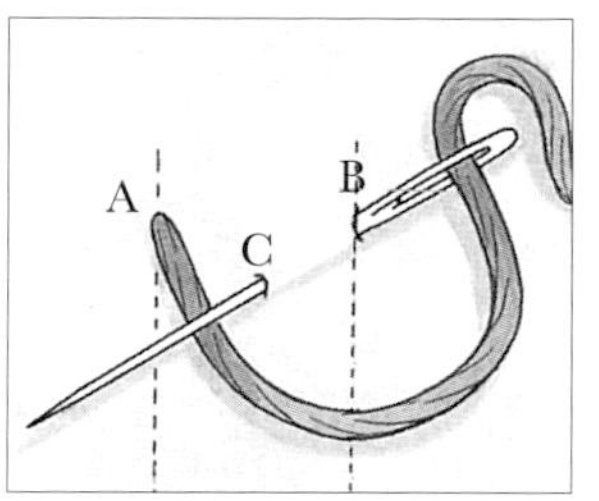

1 Come up at A, go down at B, and come up at C, keeping needle over working thread.

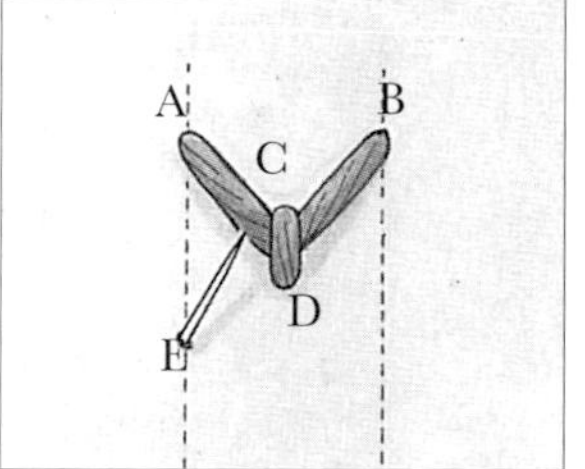

2 Go down at D, forming a small straight stitch to tie down the loop. Come up at E to begin the next stitch.

Open Loop Stitch (Variation on Fly Stitch)

This stitch is useful for depicting plant life, such as flowers, trees, ferns and branches, and for embellishment.

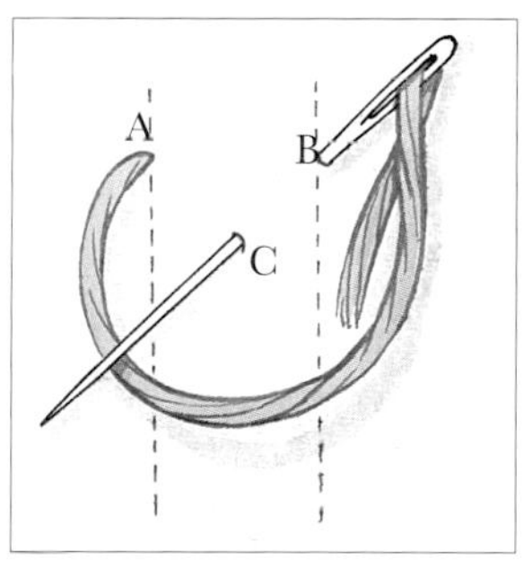

1 Come up at A and go down at B, and come up at C, keeping the needle over the working thread.

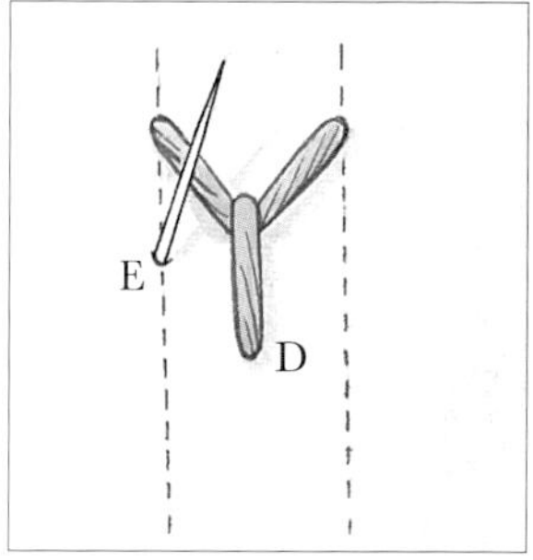

2 Go down at D, forming a long straight stitch to tie down the loop. Come up at E to begin the next stitch.

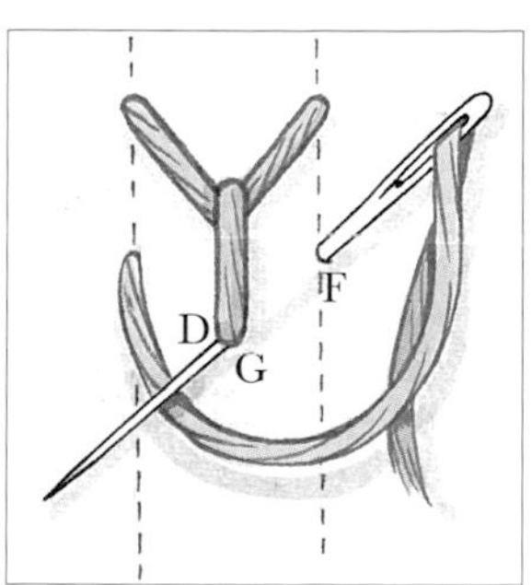

3 Go down at F to form a loop, then up at G, just beneath D. Make a long straight stitch to tie down the loop.

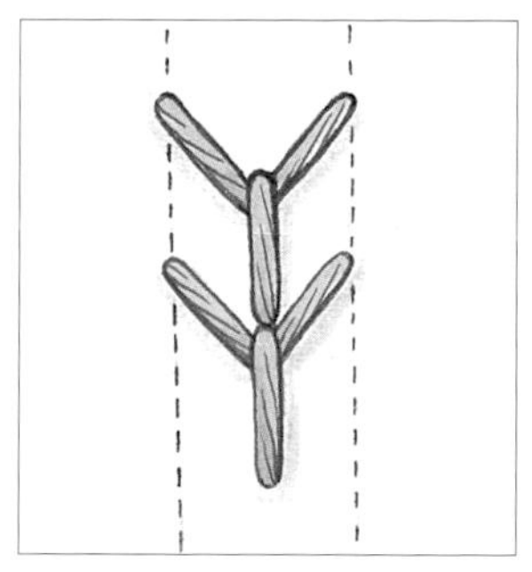

4 Continue to work down making even-sized stitches. You can vary the size of the loop to create a more irregular pattern.

Couronne Loop

Freestanding rings of thread are wrapped in tightly worked buttonhole stitches and applied as decorative elements.

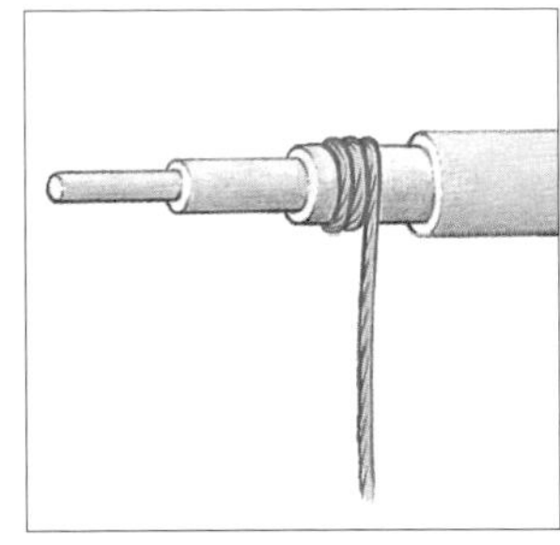

1 Wrap thread around a dowel or ring stick, two or three times. DO NOT cut the working thread.

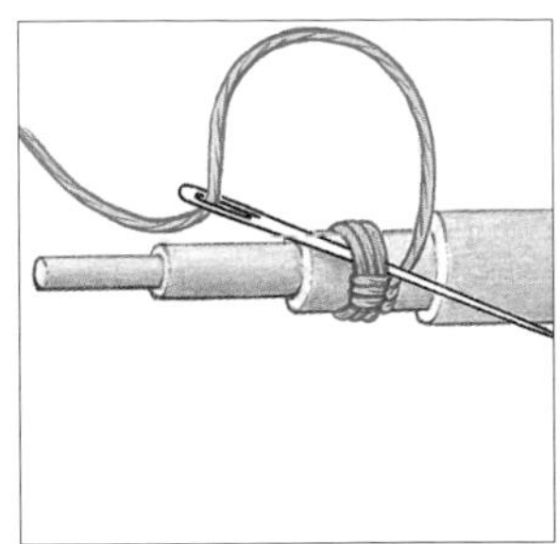

2 Using a tapestry needle, begin working buttonhole stitches over the wrapped threads.

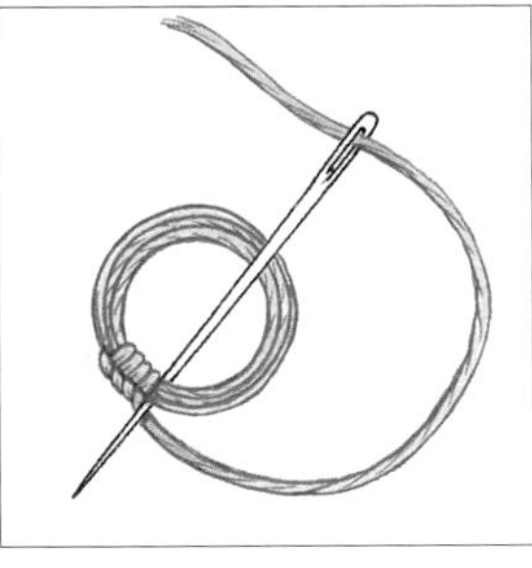

3 When the ring gets too tight to work on the stick, slip it off and continue buttonholing all the way around.

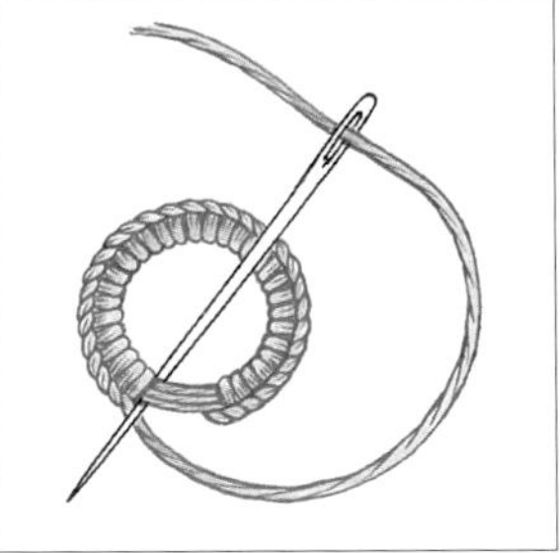

4 Finish by working the last stitch into the first one.

Combination Stitch Family

Threaded Running Stitch

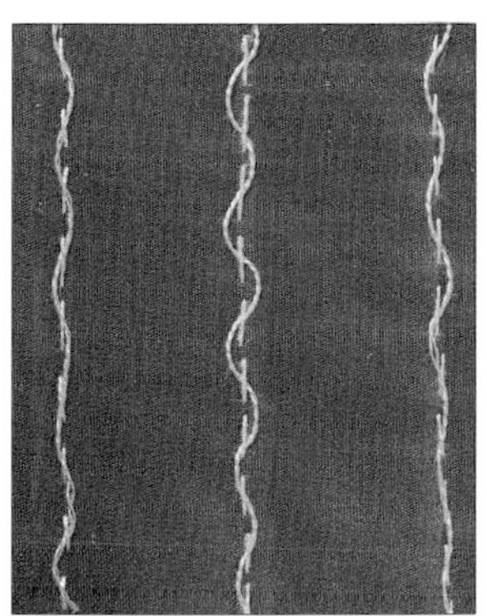

An outline stitch that creates a continuous curvy line. Double-whipped running stitch can be worked by whipping threads in both directions through each running stitch.

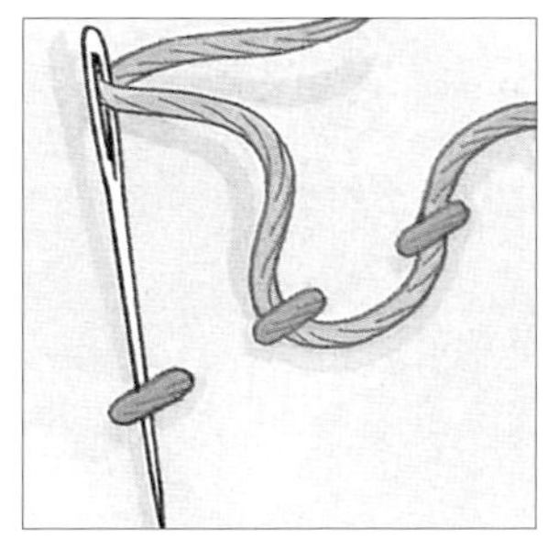

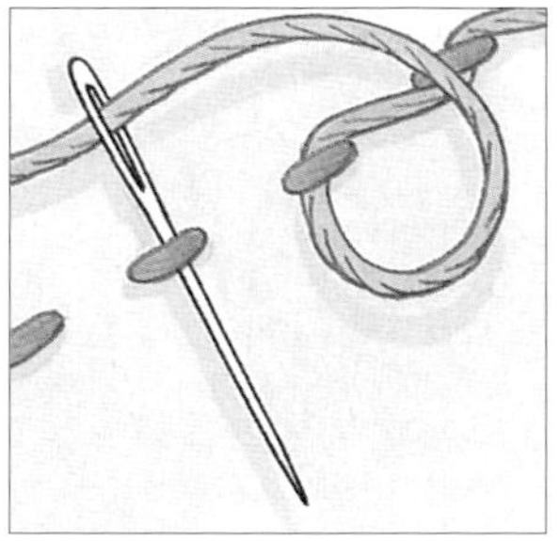

1 Work a row of running stitch (page 37). With contrasting thread, weave in and out as shown, making rounded loops. For a denser effect, work loops on both sides.

Variation
Whip in and out of each stitch, top to bottom, without picking up the background fabric.

Couching

Useful for outlining and creating unbroken straight lines, such as flower stems and grasses.

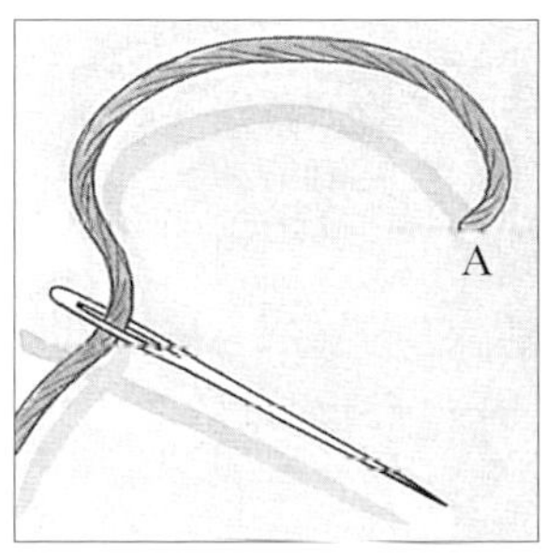

1 Bring the thread to be couched through the fabric at A.

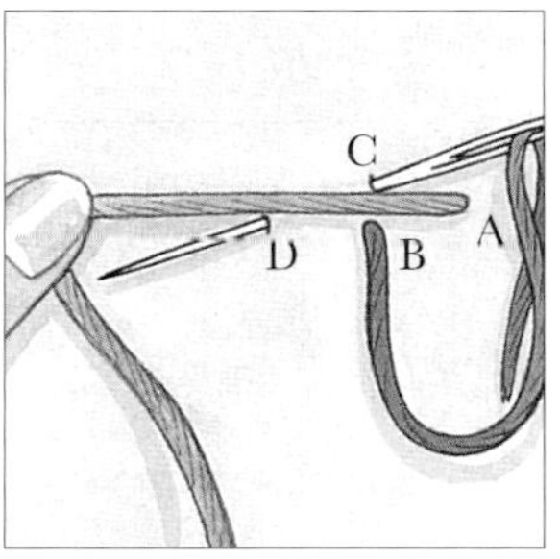

2 Bring the chosen couching thread up at B; go down at C, over the laid thread; then come up at D.

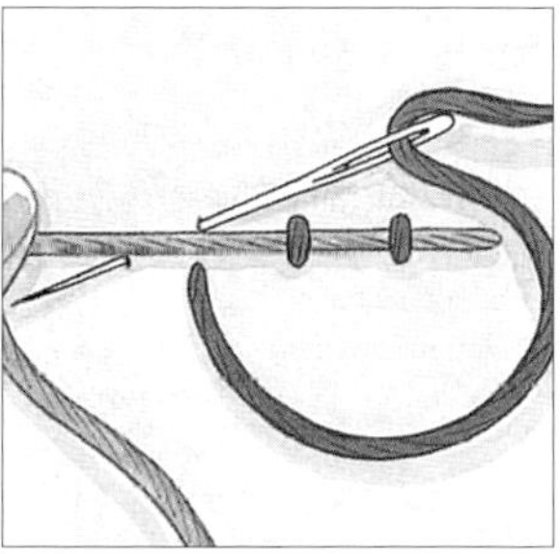

3 Repeat along the row, forming small stitches at right angles to the laid thread.

Embroideries

The Duck Pond

Inspiration for your thread paintings can be found in everyday surroundings. This charming scene of a duck pond is in the small fishing village where I live. Cretan stitch is used throughout in a spectrum of colours, with a few simple embellishments for the waterside flowers.

Materials

- Off-white pure silk backed with soft butter muslin (cheesecloth), 45 x 38 cm (18 x 14 in)
- Embroidery frame, 40 x 32 cm (16 x 12 in)
- Stapler
- Drawing paper
- Soft pencil
- Artist's brushes, nos. 10 and 12
- Watercolour paints: Winsor blue, Winsor yellow and permanent rose
- Needle
- DMC Stranded Embroidery Floss in the following colours:

  Greys: 647, 928, 3787

  Yellows: 677, 676, 973

  Blues/mauve: 775, 828, 3325, 827, 932, 931,

  Greens: 503, 320, 367, 472, 987, 704, 936

  Creams/browns: 3781, 739, 3033

  White: B5200

  Pink: 604

Stitches

1 Cretan stitch

2 Vertical Cretan stitch

3 Cretan stitch radiating from a central point

4 French knot

5 Satin stitch

6 Eyelet stitch

7 Couching

Preparation

1 Staple the silk and muslin (cheesecloth) to the wooden frame, keeping the grain of the fabric straight as it is stretched taut (see page 23).

2 Sketch your design on to a piece of drawing paper the same size as the inner edge of your frame, using the stitch diagram on page 52 as a guide. I included the row of cottages and trees in the background as they make an interesting silhouette along the horizon. When you are happy with the basic composition, transfer your design on to the silk using one of the methods described on page 25.

3 You are now ready to apply the watercolour paint. Start by painting the sky in Winsor blue, following the instructions for painting skies on page 27. Indicate the outline of the clouds with the watercolour, leaving the colour of the silk to represent the clouds themselves. When the first colour is dry, add a warm blush to the horizon with a very pale mix of permanent rose and Winsor yellow. For further information on mixing watercolours, see pages 26–27.

Stitching

4 Thread your needle with a long, single strand of dark blue. Start with a Cretan stitch 7.5–10 cm (3–4 in) long, following the line of the shadows along the horizon. Continue using Cretan stitch in pale blue to fill in the entire area of water above the bridge. Stitch over these long stitches with smaller, darker blue stitches to indicate the ripples of the water.

5 Use the same technique to work the area below the bridge, using larger stitches in the same colours to add depth. Add touches of pale mauve and white to suggest shimmering ripples in the foreground.

6 Cretan stitch can be used in different directions. With a single strand of dark grey thread, block in the silhouettes of the cottages with a small vertical stitch. Use vertical stitches in grey-green and blue thread to suggest the trees and bushes along the horizon. With a single thread, couch the two tall poles and their shadows in the water, using small Cretan stitch to form a zigzag at the base.

7 Work the rushes along the edge of the pond in vertical Cretan stitch, using one strand of thread in a variety of rich, leafy greens. Use a dark grey for the shadows. Indicate the reflection of the bushes in the water with dark blue and green thread.

8 Next, fill in the top of the bridge with Cretan stitch in beige thread. Use vertical Cretan stitch in a range of brown and grey tones to suggest the rough stone sides and the stonework of the arch. Use a dark blue Cretan stitch for the shadow beneath the arch.

9 Wild flowers and grasses add texture to the foreground. Using two strands of thread, stitch a background of rich green grasses in vertical Cretan stitch. Couch tall, dark reeds bending across the water with one strand of dark green or brown thread. Add French knots to suggest seedheads.

10 With a bright, cheerful yellow, add some more French knots at the water's edge. I used eyelet stitch to suggest small pink flowers, and Cretan stitch radiating from a central point for the white daisies. Use similar techniques to add the remaining groups of flowers, varying their size to give a sense of depth to the picture.

11 Complete the tranquil scene with some mallard ducks worked in satin stitch in the foreground and a suggestion of ducks in the background, embroidered with just a few fine stitches in soft grey thread.

WATERCOLOUR SKY

You can achieve a beautifully graded sky with careful washes of watercolour. Apply the paint loosely, letting the soft edges of colour define the shapes of the clouds. Finish with a few simple Cretan stitches to give depth and texture.

Sailing Boats

This tranquil coastal scene is stitched almost entirely in Cretan stitch. The colourful yacht in the foreground takes pride of place, its vertical mast cutting through the horizontal rows of Cretan stitch.

STITCHES

1 Cretan stitch

2 Vertical Cretan stitch

3 Couching

Materials

- Off-white pure silk backed with soft butter muslin (cheesecloth), 35 x 40 cm (14 x 15 in)
- Embroidery frame, 30 x 34 cm (12 x 13 in)
- Stapler
- Drawing paper
- Soft pencil
- Artist's brushes, nos. 10 and 12
- Watercolour paints: Winsor blue, Winsor yellow and permanent rose
- Needle
- Thin cardboard
- DMC Metallic Cotton Pearl in the following colours:

  Gold/Silver: 5282, 5283
- DMC Stranded Embroidery Floss in the following colours:

  Greys: 318, 3023, 535

  Yellows/oranges: 3823, 725, 951, 3770

  Blues/mauve: 775, 3756, 322, 3325, 3042

  Cream/brown: 422, 898

  Green: 730

  White: B5200

Preparation

1 Staple the silk and muslin (cheesecloth) to the wooden frame, keeping the grain of the fabric straight as it is stretched taut (see page 23).

2 Sketch your basic design on to a piece of drawing paper the same size as the inner edge of your frame, using the stitch diagram on page 56 as a guide. I focused on the church and the trees, which make an interesting shape along the horizon. Note how a space is left to accommodate the sailing boat in the foreground. When you are happy with the basic composition, transfer your design on to the silk using one of the methods described on page 25.

3 You are now ready to apply the watercolour paint. Start by painting the sky using Winsor blue, following the instructions for painting skies on page 27. This is a very intense colour, so test the shade on a scrap of silk first. The wash will appear lighter when it dries. Indicate the outline of the clouds with the paint, leaving the colour of the silk to represent the clouds themselves. When the first colour is dry, add a warm blush to the horizon with a very pale mix of permanent rose and Winsor yellow.

Stitching

4 Thread your needle with a long, single strand of pale yellow embroidery floss. Start with Cretan stitch 10–12 cm (4–5 in) long, following the line of the horizon. Continue using Cretan stitch to fill in the area of water in front of the trees. Couch down these long stitches with smaller, dark cream stitches to indicate ripples in the water.

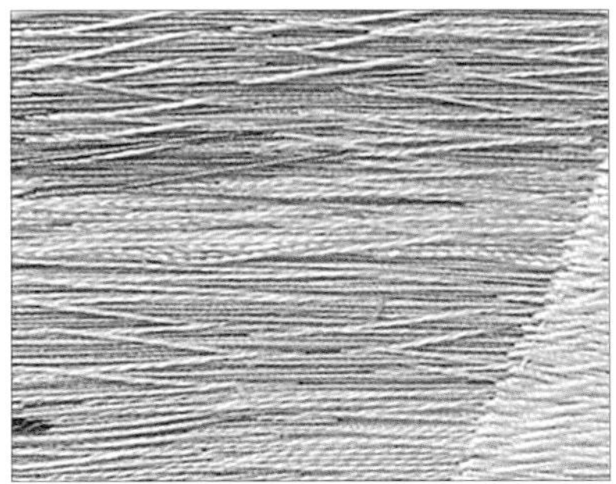

5 Highlight the clouds with a smaller Cretan stitch in shades of grey, cream and yellow to tone with the colours of the water.

6 Use the same technique to work the blue expanse of sea in the foreground. Again, start with the palest colour thread, then introduce darker shades and smaller stitches for increased depth. Finish with touches of deep blue and dark brown on the left-hand side of the picture to give balance and variety.

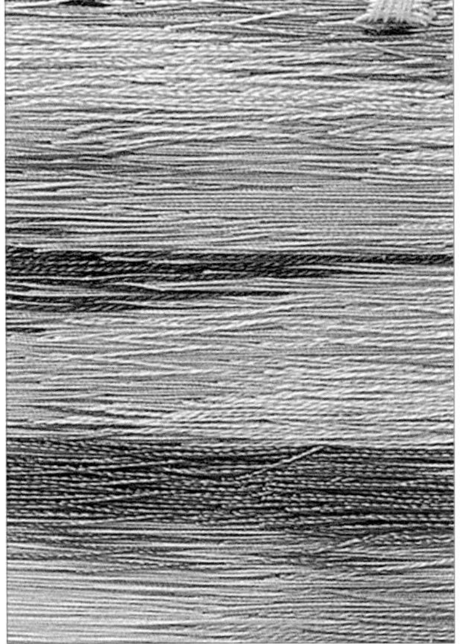

7 Cretan stitch can be used in different directions. With a single strand of dark grey thread, block in the silhouette of the church with a small vertical stitch. Use vertical stitches in grey-green and mauve thread to suggest the trees and bushes along the horizon.

8 The sailing boats are superimposed over the embroidered sea, enriching and bringing the pleasant seascape to life. First make a template of the large yacht out of cardboard and cut out the shape. Pin the template in position and outline the shape with a small running stitch. Block in the solid areas of the sails with horizontal Cretan stitch using two strands of thread in white and yellow, then stitch the shadows on the water in the same colours, with zigzag Cretan stitch. Note how a few gold and silver threads sparkle in the water, creating a shimmering reflection of the sails. Couch the mast with a single strand of dark brown thread, then stitch the base of the boat and the two figures in vertical Cretan stitch, using dark grey thread.

9 Complete the tranquil scene with some small yachts in the distance, created in horizontal and vertical Cretan stitch in white, grey and blue.

RECESSION

Recession is emphasized by the size of the boats in the background. Note how they have been spaced at irregular intervals to create an interesting pattern in the water. One dark sail leads the eye through the picture to the distant church.

Down the Lane

A portrayal of a country scene, inviting a walk towards the church and the cluster of cottages in the distance. The play of light and shade inspired me to reproduce this charming landscape. Once again, I used my favourite method of making sketches on site before transferring the simple composition to silk.

Materials

- Cream pure silk backed with soft butter muslin (cheesecloth), 35 x 40 cm (14 x 15 in)
- Embroidery frame, 30 x 34 cm (12 x 13 in)
- Stapler
- Drawing paper
- Soft pencil
- Artist's brushes, nos. 10 and 12
- Watercolour paints: Winsor blue, Winsor yellow and permanent rose
- Needle
- DMC Stranded Embroidery Floss in the following colours:

  Greens: 904, 3345, 895, 704, 907, 906, 989, 472

  Greys: 648, 3072, 762

  Blues: 826, 825

  Pinks: 894, 818, 892

  Creams/browns: 712, 437, 951, 839, 898

  Orange/peach: 356, 977, 351, 754

  White: B5200

STITCHES

1 Cretan stitch

2 Straight stitch

3 French knot

4 Vertical Cretan stitch

Preparation

1 Staple the silk and muslin (cheesecloth) to the wooden frame, keeping the grain of the fabric straight as it is stretched taut (see page 23).

2 Using the stitch diagram opposite as a guide, draw the abstract shapes on to a piece of drawing paper the same size as the inner edge of your frame. You may wish to include the outline of the tree and the path, plus the line of the horizon. Omit the buildings at this stage. Cut out the shapes individually, like the pieces of a jigsaw, and draw around them on the silk fabric.

3 You are now ready to apply the watercolour paint. Start by painting the sky with very diluted Winsor blue. This is an intense colour, so test the strength first on a scrap of silk fabric. The wash will appear lighter when it dries. Indicate the outline of the clouds with the watercolour, leaving the colour of the silk to represent the clouds themselves.

4 When the blue paint is dry, add a warm blush to the horizon with a very pale mix of permanent rose and Winsor yellow. For more information on mixing watercolours and painting skies, see page 27.

Stitching

5 Start by working the irregular background shape behind the leaves of the tree, using horizontal Cretan stitch in long, varying lengths. Use two strands of thread in shades of dark green and brown, keeping the stitches close together to form a solid foundation for the leaves and branches. Work the tree trunk in the same stitch, using darker shades of green and brown.

6 Select a range of bright, light greens for the leaves. Using one strand of thread only, work the fan-shaped clusters of leaves in Cretan stitch so that they couch down the long horizontal background stitches. Note how the individual stitches of each leaf radiate out from a central point to form a miniature fan shape. Follow the picture for the positioning of the leaves. Note how the leaves are smaller and less densely spaced as they reach the tips of the branches. Work the branches in long straight stitch using two strands of dark brown thread.

7 Observe the play of light on the distant field and indicate this using horizontal Cretan stitch in a range of light yellow-greens. Use one strand of thread only in your needle and make your stitches 1.5–2.5 cm (¾–1 in) long.

8 The path is also stitched in horizontal Cretan stitch, this time using the palest cream. Note how the whole of the path is completed before the shadows are superimposed in a darker shade (see Step 10).

9 Stitch the dark green meadow on the left-hand side of the path using the full range of dark green threads. First create a foundation of dark green horizontal Cretan stitch, 2.5–5 cm (1–2 in) long, using two strands of thread. Then superimpose the smaller, lighter coloured stitches over the top, using one strand of thread only. Add a few straight, vertical stitches in brown to indicate a fence dividing the two meadows.

10 Work the meadow on the right-hand side of the picture in the same colours, to create a backdrop for the lighter green grasses and clusters of flowers.

11 The next step is to introduce the play of light. Study the picture closely as it is important to get the shafts of sunlight in the appropriate places. Begin with one strand of dark grey thread and horizontal Cretan stitch. Work the dark areas of the path in grey and blue, over the cream background colour to create a series of strong shadows running across the path. Continue the shadows on to the left-hand bank, but change to a dark green, working the stitches at a slight angle to suggest the rising bank. Repeat the effect on the opposite side of the path, underneath the tree. Now take a golden ochre and indicate the patches of sunlight in the foreground using one strand of thread. Once again, continue the shaft of light on to the meadows on either side of the path, following the picture carefully.

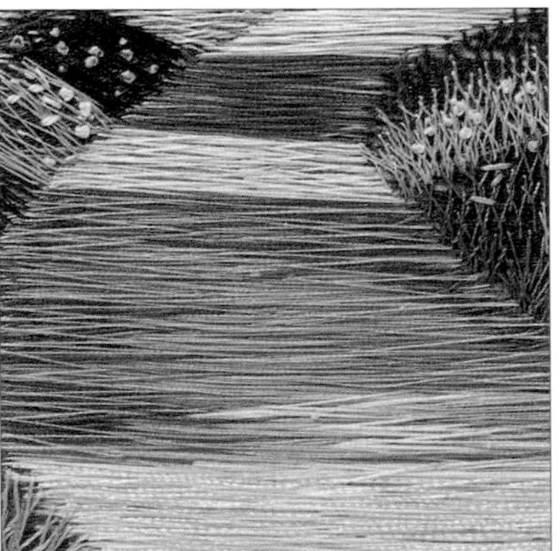

12 The clumps of grasses are superimposed over the embroidered meadows in vertical Cretan stitch, to make them more prominent. Choose a variety of light greens, avoiding the very light green of the distant meadow or you will reduce its impact.

13 The flowers are embroidered French knots, created using two strands of white thread. Note how the flowers in the foreground are large, with dark green stems, while the flowers in the back ground are smaller and paler in comparison. Use one strand of very pale grey thread for the flowers in the shadows. This will help to emphasize the play of light and shade and also direct the eye towards the distant church on the horizon.

14 Indicate the buildings along the horizon in pencil using simple, abstract shapes, such as squares or rectangles. Work the roofs in horizontal Cretan stitch, using one strand of pink or orange thread. Work the church in medium grey, keeping the stitches small and compact. Indicate the windows with a tiny, grey straight stitch. Stitch the distant bushes on either side of the buildings in small vertical Cretan stitch, using one strand of thread in soft blue and green.

15 The finishing touch is to add a few irregular horizontal Cretan stitches in a peach colour to the expanse of sky directly above the buildings.

LIGHT AND SHADE

The play of light and shade is an important feature of this landscape. Note how I have incorporated a wide range of colours – from pure white, through pale cream, to very dark green – in order to highlight the deep shadows underneath the tree and the bright shafts of sunlight that run across the path.

Gone Fishing

Two snugly dressed fishermen form the focus of this tranquil river scene, which is worked almost entirely in Cretan stitch. The water is stitched in shades of mauve and blue, with pale cream in the foreground to reflect the colour of the sky.

STITCHES

1 Cretan stitch

2 Vertical Cretan stitch

3 Couching

4 French knot

Materials

- Off-white pure silk backed with soft butter muslin (cheesecloth), 35 x 40 cm (14 x 15 in)
- Embroidery frame, 30 x 34 cm (12 x 13 in)
- Stapler
- Drawing paper
- Soft pencil
- Artist's brushes, nos. 10 and 12
- Watercolour paints: Winsor blue, Winsor yellow and permanent rose
- Needle
- DMC Stranded Embroidery Floss in the following colours:

  Greens: 3347, 3346, 3813, 927, 928, 904, 907, 3348, 703

  Blues/mauves: 775, 798, 3756, 3942, 3841, 3836, 211

  Yellows: 676, 677, 3822

  Red: 349

  Brown: 898

  White/cream: B5200, 746

Preparation

1 Staple the silk and muslin (cheesecloth) to the wooden frame, keeping the grain of the fabric straight as it is stretched taut (see page 23).

2 Sketch your basic design on to a piece of drawing paper the same size as the inner edge of your frame, using the stitch diagram on page 66 as a guide. You might want to include the cottages, riverbank and bushes on the horizon, and the two figures and the clumps of reeds in the water. When you are happy with the basic composition, transfer the line of the riverbank, the cottages and the bushes on to the silk using one of the methods described on page 25. There is no need to transfer the figures and reeds as these are superimposed over the embroidered water.

3 You are now ready to apply the watercolour paint. Start by painting the early-morning sky with a wash of very pale cream, made by mixing Winsor yellow with a touch of permanent rose. Mix a pale mauve the same colour as the sea from Winsor blue, permanent rose and a touch of Winsor yellow. Test the colour on a scrap of fabric, and paint the still-damp area of the sky in the appropriate places. For further information on mixing watercolours, see page 26.

Stitching

4 Start with the green riverbank on the horizon. Thread your needle with a long, single strand of moss green thread and, using long Cretan stitch, 10–12 cm (4–5 in) in length, fill in the area of riverbank below the trees. Couch down these long stitches with smaller, dark green stitches.

5 Use the same technique, and pale blues and mauves, to work the water in front of the riverbed, couching down the long stitches with smaller stitches in a darker shade. When the pale blue and mauve areas are complete, introduce additional open Cretan stitch in white to suggest light playing on the water. Finish with a warm cream in the foreground to reflect the colour of the sky, again overstitching with shimmering white. Note how the superimposed Cretan stitches tying down the long stitches are smaller towards the distance and larger and more open towards the foreground, creating perspective.

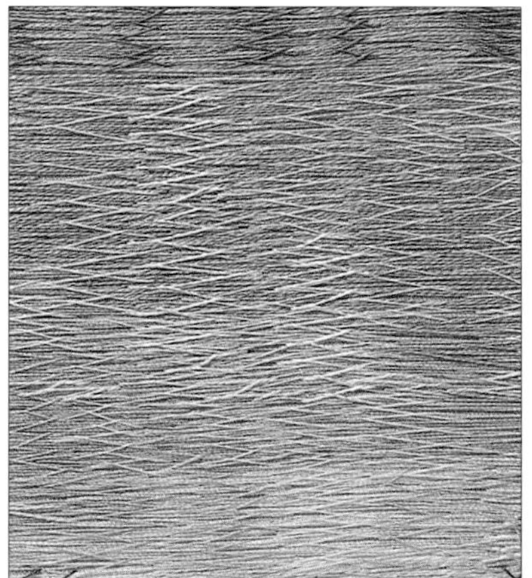

6 Cretan stitch can be used in different directions. With two strands of brick-red thread, block in the roofs of the cottages in horizontal Cretan stitch, then work the chimneys in vertical Cretan stitch using the same colour thread.

Work the trees and bushes along the horizon in vertical Cretan stitch, using a single strand of grey-green or grey-blue thread. Then work the clumps of French knots in similar shades of grey and green.

7 The clumps of reeds in the foreground are embroidered over the water in long Cretan stitch using one strand of thread. Use rich, leafy shades of green for the leaves, varying the direction of each clump to suggest the reeds blowing in the wind, and dark green for the French knots at the base. Indicate the reflection of the reeds in the water with zigzag Cretan stitch, using a single strand of dark green thread.

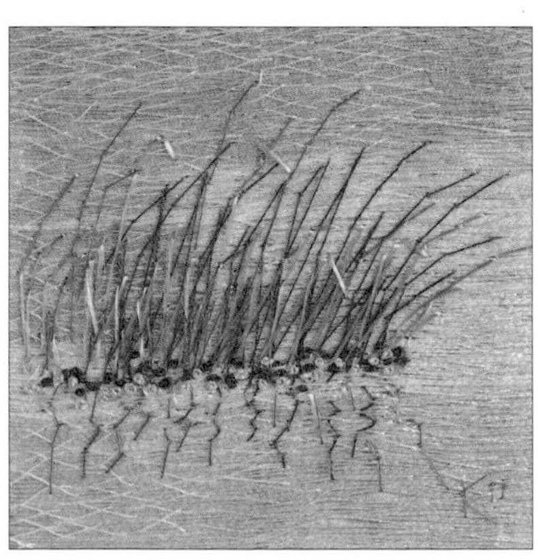

8 The two figures are superimposed over the embroidered water to give them a three-dimensional appearance. For best results, choose colours that contrast with the river and block in the shapes with a small, horizontal Cretan stitch. I chose a brick-red jacket for one fisherman and a red hat for the other, to link the figures to the red roofs of the cottages on the horizon. Your figures do not need to look like mine. Be yourself. Stick men or childish drawings both have an appeal. The reflections in the water are also created in Cretan stitch, but they are more vague in colour and outline. Finish with a few cream Cretan stitches worked over the top of the reflections to suggest ripples in the water.

9 The fishermen are standing on a small jetty which is couched in dark brown, using three strands of thread. The fishing rods are also couched, this time using a single strand of thread. Echo the shape of the rods in the water using small Cretan stitch to form a zigzag at the base. Finish up by stitching the two buckets in bright yellow and green thread, using small horizontal Cretan stitch.

Drawing figures

Don't be daunted by drawing the fishermen. Consider them as squares of abstract shapes. Be careful not to make the heads too big, and make sure that their jackets are large and padded enough to provide protection against the sea breeze.

Pansy Faces

I draw some inspiration for my thread paintings from my garden. For this embroidery, I selected a cluster of pansies and grasses, which I floated in a saucer of water to keep them fresh while I painted them on the pure silk.

Materials

- Cream pure silk backed with soft butter muslin (cheesecloth), 45 x 38 cm (18 x 14 in)
- Embroidery frame, 40 x 32 cm (16 x 12 in)
- Stapler
- Drawing paper
- Soft pencil
- Artist's brushes, nos. 10 and 12
- Watercolour paints:
  Winsor blue, Winsor yellow and permanent rose
- Needle
- Closely-woven cotton fabric for backing the trapunto areas
- A little cotton wadding (batting)
- 1.5 mm (1/8 in) satin embroidery ribbon in blue, white and mauve
- White patterned lace for the butterfly
- White cardboard (postcard weight)
- PVA glue
- DMC Stranded Embroidery Floss in the following colours:
  Greens: 320, 907, 3819
  Purples/blues: 333, 800 3840, 553, 3834
  Pinks/reds: 605, 3607
  Yellows/orange: 743, 3823 973, 972

Stitches

1 Cretan stitch
2 Couching
3 Detached chain stitch
4 French knot
5 Straight stitch
6 Zigzag chain stitch
7 Satin stitch
8 Bullion knot
9 Open loop stitch

Kit Nicol

Preparation

1 Staple the silk and muslin (cheesecloth) to the wooden frame, keeping the grain of the fabric straight as it is stretched taut (see page 23).

2 Sketch the basic design on to a piece of drawing paper the same size as the inner edge of your frame, using the stitch diagram on page 70 as a guide. Transfer your design to the silk using one of the methods described on page 25.

3 Paint the pansy flowers in your chosen colours – I chose a mauve shade, which I created by mixing Winsor blue with permanent rose, for the two pansies in the background, and Winsor yellow with a touch of permanent rose for the pansies in the foreground.

4 When the pansies are dry, paint the backgrounds in contrasting shades. I chose clear blue around the yellow pansies and pale yellow drifting to pink behind the lilac pansies. I intentionally allowed the background colours to run into each other and mingle on the surface of the fabric. When the backgrounds are dry, paint the leaves and grasses in shades of green, using a delicate touch for some of them, to suggest shadows.

Stitching

5 Begin with the pansies. I started by creating a border around the outside of each pansy with Cretan stitch. I used two strands of thread for the outer border and one strand of thread for the inner bands of Cretan stitch. Select five or six toning colours for each flower and follow the photograph carefully. I used shades of blue, pink, mauve and purple for the lilac pansies, and golden yellows, oranges and purples for the yellow flowers. Note how the brighter yellow pansy on the far right has little touches of pink as an accent to pick up the pink tints of the background. When you are happy with the detail of the petals, work the centres in bullion knots, using three strands of thread in a variety of pleasing colours.

6 The large pansy leaves are outlined with a single row of couching, using two strands of green or mustard yellow. The veins on the leaves and most of the stems are also couched, but note how I have left some of the stems free of embroidery to give a delicate, wispy appearance.

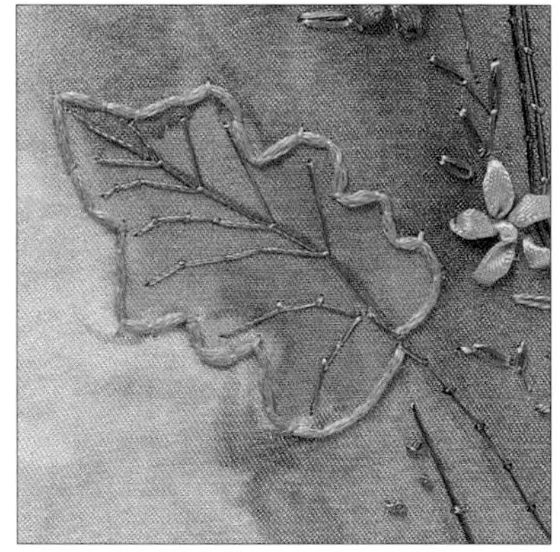

7 Work the delicate seedheads in mustard yellow, using detached chain stitch and two strands of thread. Embroider the ears of corn using zigzag chain stitch and two strands of golden yellow thread.

8 The open pansies and some of their leaves are padded in the trapunto technique to give a three-dimensional appearance. Cut a piece of cotton large enough to cover your chosen areas and follow the instructions for trapunto on page 28.

9 The clusters of miniature daisies are worked in satin embroidery ribbon in three colours. Work the petals first in straight stitch, varying the size and shape of each flower for a natural look. Then work the French knots in the centre, using three strands of bright yellow.

10 The final touch is to add the butterfly in the top left-hand corner. First cut the wings from patterned lace and back with thin white cardboard, gluing them into place with PVA glue. Then introduce a little colour on the wings with pale blue watercolour to give a two-tone effect. Arrange the wings on the silk, overlapping them slightly for a three-dimensional effect, and stitch down securely using pale blue thread for the satin stitch body.

STITCHING

I have used a wide range of embroidery stitches and several different tones of the same colour to introduce depth and bring the flowers to life.

Sunflowers

These cheerful sunflowers are padded in the trapunto technique, which brings them to life. Note how the contrasting purple background highlights the glowing yellow and orange of the petals.

Materials

- Off-white pure silk backed with soft butter muslin (cheesecloth), 45 x 38 cm (18 x 14 in)
- Embroidery frame, 40 x 32 cm (16 x 12 in)
- Stapler
- Drawing paper
- Soft pencil
- Artist's brushes, nos. 10 and 12
- Watercolour paints: Winsor blue, Winsor yellow and permanent rose
- Needle
- Closely-woven cotton fabric for backing the trapunto areas
- A little cotton wadding (batting)
- Grey-green organza ribbon, 8 mm (1/4 in) wide
- Tiny purple sequins
- DMC Stranded Embroidery Floss in the following colours:

  Browns: 3859, 3858

  Greens: 564, 772, 472, 907, 959

  Blues/purples: 827, 931, 340, 3835

  Yellows/orange: 3823, 973, 677, 725, 972, 971

Stitches

1 Couching

2 Seed stitch

3 Open loop stitch

4 Cretan stitch

5 French knot

6 Eyelet stitch

Kit Nicol 1999

Preparation

1 Staple the silk and muslin (cheesecloth) to the wooden frame, keeping the grain of the fabric straight as it is stretched taut (see page 23).

2 Sketch your basic design on to a piece of drawing paper the same size as the inner edge of your frame, using the stitch diagram on page 74 as a guide. When you are happy with the basic composition, transfer your design on to the silk using one of the methods described on page 25.

3 You are now ready to apply the watercolour paint. Start by painting the sunflower petals in different shades of yellow, for a natural effect. I intentionally allowed the colours to run into each other and mingle on the surface of the fabric. When the yellow paint is dry, add a warm purple in the centre of each flower. Paint the leaves and stems in shades of green and yellow, following the instructions for mixing watercolours on page 26.

4 The background is painted a rich purple to contrast with the colour of the petals. Mix up a warm purple and carefully apply it around your flowers.

Stitching

5 Many of the sunflower petals are padded in the trapunto technique to give them a three-dimensional appearance. Cut a piece of cotton fabric the same size as the silk and tack (baste) in place on the muslin (cheesecloth) backing. Select groups of petals and outline them first with a small running stitch in a matching colour, then pad lightly with wadding (batting), following the directions on page 28. Treat the large leaves in the foreground in the same way as the petals, padding them to make them three-dimensional.

6 You are now ready to outline the individual petals with couching, using two strands of thread, stitched down with one strand in a matching colour. Use the full range of yellows, matching the shade to the painted silk. Emphasize some of the petals with open loop stitch, using two strands of yellow and orange.

7 Treat the leaf towards the top of the design in the same way as the petals, using open loop stitch in pale blue and green threads to introduce depth and texture.

8 Outline the remaining leaves and their veins with couching using two strands of blue-green thread, stitched down with one strand in a matching colour. Then work the areas of seed stitch, Cretan stitch and open loop stitch, following the stitch diagram on page 74.

9 Introduce further texture to the thread painting by stitching a small frill of organza ribbon over the calyx of two of the flowers.

10 Couch some of the flower stems using six strands of blue-green thread, tied down with one strand in a matching colour.

11 The flower centres are made up of tiny sequins, stitched in an irregular pattern to provide variety and interest. Pick up three, four or five sequins at a time, on your needle and stitch them in place. Surround with French knots in a matching colour, made using three strands of thread.

12 The final stage is to embellish the purple background with surface texture using eyelet holes and painted circles, spaced at irregular intervals to create an interesting pattern. Begin each eyelet stitch by puncturing the silk fabric with a thick needle. Thread your sewing needle with one or two strands of blue or purple thread and use straight stitch in irregular lengths to surround the hole and form an attractive star shape. Complete the stitch painting by adding very tiny circles, painted in watercolour, mingling them through the stitchery to please the eye and create an attractive rhythm.

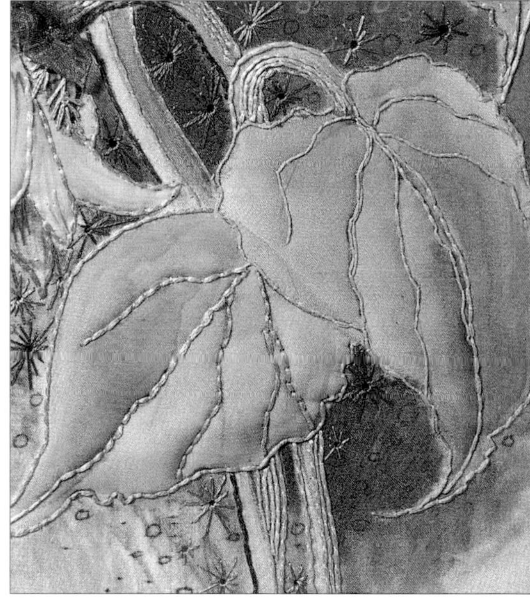

TEXTURAL EFFECTS

The painted leaves are padded in the trapunto technique and then embellished with stitching to give them a realistic three-dimensional finish.

Raised Embroideries

Spanish Garden

The glorious colours and textures of this garden in Spain inspired me to introduce tropical flowers into my thread paintings. To enrich the painting, I made the chair three-dimensional and padded the hat and pots.

STITCHES

1 Bullion knot
2 Open buttonhole stitch
3 Couching
4 French knot
5 Herringbone stitch
6 Leaf stitch
7 Open loop stitch
8 Running stitch
9 Satin stitch
10 Star stitch
11 Cretan stitch
12 Straight stitch

MATERIALS

- Off-white pure silk backed with soft butter muslin (cheesecloth), 35 x 40 cm (14 x 15 in)
- Embroidery frame, 30 x 34 cm (12 x 13 in)
- Stapler
- Drawing paper
- Soft pencil
- Artist's brushes, nos. 10 and 12
- Watercolour paints: Winsor blue, Winsor yellow and permanent rose
- Needle
- Closely-woven cotton fabric for backing the trapunto areas
- A little cotton wadding (batting)
- A few florist's medium-gauge stub wires
- White embroidery silk or fine crochet cotton
- Thin cardboard (postcard weight)
- Satin fabric for the chair cushion and hat
- PVA glue
- DMC Stranded Embroidery Floss in the following colours:

  GREENS: 369 562, 472, 987, 501, 966, 471

  PINKS/REDS: 3801, 3706, 224, 352

  PURPLES/BLUE: 327, 554, 809

  YELLOW/ORANGE: 973, 971

  GREY: 451, 453, 646

  WHITE: B5200

Preparation

1 Staple the silk and muslin (cheesecloth) to the wooden frame, keeping the grain of the fabric straight as it is stretched taut (see page 23).

2 Sketch the basic design on to a piece of drawing paper the same size as the inner edge of your frame, using the stitch diagram on page 80 as a guide. Try to keep your design simple, basing it around the key elements of the chair, the pots of flowers and the palm tree. When you are happy with the basic composition, transfer your design on to the silk using one of the methods described on page 25.

3 You are now ready to apply the watercolour paint. Start by applying a pale wash of Winsor blue over the sky area, using the larger brush. When this is dry, introduce a light sandy-coloured wash to the foreground, leaving the white silk visible for the smaller pots. Mix a pale terracotta colour and use to paint the large pot. When dry, introduce some shadows on the pot with a deeper shade, made by adding a little blue to your paint mixture. For further information on mixing water-colours, see page 26.

4 When the background colours are dry, paint the flowers and plants in the garden. Some of these can be quite faint and blurred, to give an impression of depth once the embroidery is in place. For best results, use fairly dry paint to prevent the colours from running into the silk.

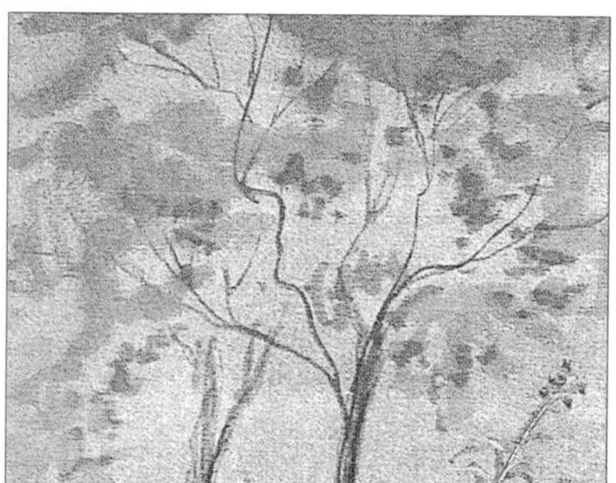

Stitching

5 This piece uses a variety of stitches to capture the exquisite textures of the flowers. Working from right to left, start by embroidering the flower border in the background, using one or two strands of thread. Either follow the stitch diagram on page 80 or introduce your own choice of stitches.

6 You can now embroider a bounty of flowers in the pots. The white star-stitch daisies are finished with a yellow French knot in the centre. French knots in shades of blue and green are also used to suggest a profusion of foliage. Satin stitch is perfectly suited to the flat leaves of the cactus. See the stitch diagram, or use your own stitch combinations.

7 The three flowerpots, including their embroidered flowers, are padded in the trapunto technique to give them increased prominence. Start by cutting a piece of cotton fabric large enough to cover the areas to be padded, then follow the instructions for trapunto on page 28.

8 Prepare the pieces of wire for the chair by wrapping them with white embroidery silk or fine crochet cotton (see page 30). Make a template of the chair from cardboard and bend the wires to fit the shape. You should end up with an elaborate wrought-iron design. Bend the arms forward to give a three-dimensional effect and stitch the chair invisibly on to the silk. Embellish with French knots and little circles of satin stitch.

9 Make a cardboard template of the cushion and use to cut out a shape from satin, making it slightly larger than the template all round. Cut an oval of wadding (batting) the same size as the template. Assemble the two layers (see page 29), then decorate with a pattern of polka dots in Winsor blue paint. Slipstitch the cushion to the chair, outlining the edges with couching.

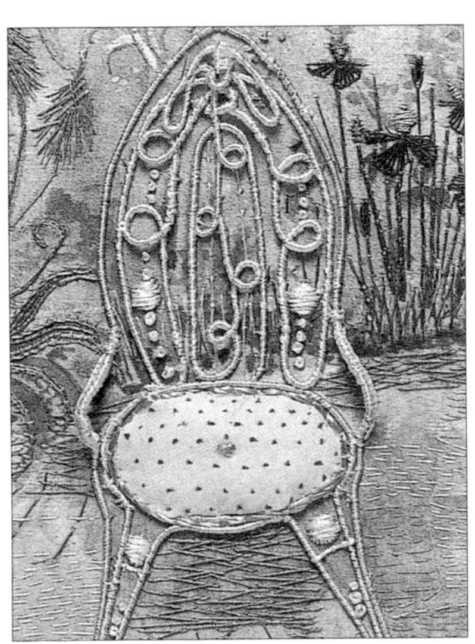

10 Make up the hat from satin fabric in the same way as the cushion (see page 29) and stitch in place on the silk background. Work the ribbon around the brim of the hat in straight stitch and the rose using a cluster of bullion knots.

11 To complete the thread painting, embroider the shadows beneath the chair and in front of the pots with pale grey Cretan stitch. Then introduce the texture on the paving stones, using running stitch in shades of grey.

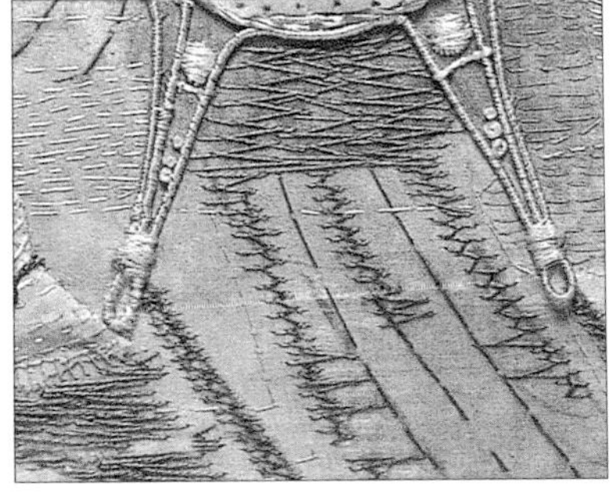

Depth and texture

To add depth and texture to the palm tree, I first painted the leaves with a fine brush and then stitched over some of them with open loop stitch, leaving a background tracery of painted leaves.

The Cake Shop

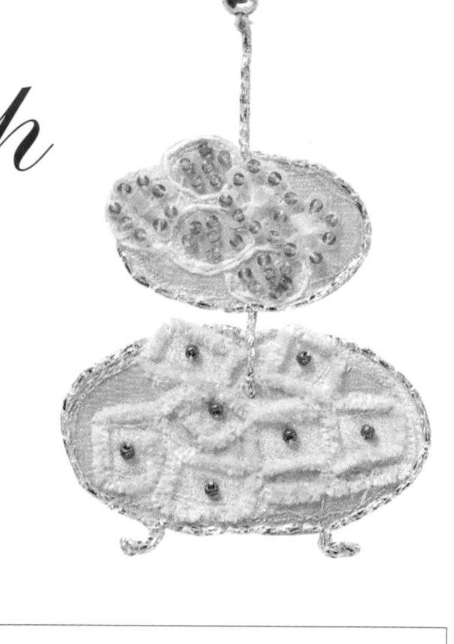

This thread painting tells the story of two small children looking through the window of a cake shop at the mouthwatering display of cakes and buns inside.

STITCHES

1 Running stitch

2 French knot

3 Seed stitch

4 Straight stitch

5 Couching

6 Closed buttonhole stitch

7 Detached buttonhole stitch

Materials

- Cream pure silk backed with soft butter muslin (cheesecloth), 35 x 40 cm (14 x 15 in)
- Embroidery frame, 30 x 34 cm (12 x 13 in)
- Stapler
- Drawing paper
- Soft pencil
- Thin cardboard (postcard weight)
- Artist's brushes, nos. 10 and 12
- Watercolour paints: Winsor blue, Winsor yellow and permanent rose
- White gouache paint
- Needle
- Closely-woven cotton fabric for backing the trapunto areas
- A little cotton wadding (batting)
- Miniature sequins in assorted colours
- Small glass beads in assorted shapes and colours
- Chenille thread in white and cream
- Felt in peach, skin-coloured pink, sugar pink, pale orange and white
- Cream ribbon, 3 mm (1/4 in) wide
- Skin-coloured silk satin
- A few florist's medium-gauge stub wires
- DMC Metallic Cotton Pearl in silver (5283)
- DMC Cotton Pearl in the following colours:

  PINK: 819

  YELLOW/WHITE: 3078, B5200

  GREEN: 702

  CREAM/BROWNS: 738, 938, 644

  BLUE/PURPLE: 809, 327
- DMC Stranded Embroidery Floss in the following colours:

  GREEN: 890

  CREAM/BEIGE: 822, 842

  PINK: 818

  GREY: 762

Preparation

1 Staple the silk and muslin (cheesecloth) to the wooden frame, keeping the grain of the fabric straight as it is stretched taut (see page 23).

2 Sketch your basic design on to a piece of paper the same size as the inner edge of your frame, using the diagram on page 84 as a guide. Transfer the design to the silk, omitting the people. Make a full-size cardboard template of the four figures and arrange them on the silk. Lightly draw around the shapes with a soft pencil. Draw in the detail of the stonework in the foreground.

3 You are now ready to apply the watercolour paint. Start by mixing a pale cream and use to paint the top quarter of the picture above the shelves. Now mix a pale grey and use to paint the shadows underneath the shelves. The counter is painted a very pale blue to offset the colour of the cakes. Be careful not to make it too dark. Finish with a pale terracotta wash over the lower quarter of the picture, to form a background for the stonework. When the background colours are dry, take your smallest brush and carefully outline the horizontal lines of the shelves in pale grey. Use the same colour to indicate the vertical lines of the tongue-and-groove panelling. Further information on mixing watercolours can be found on page 26.

4 You can now paint the till, the groceries on the shelves and the items on the counter in your chosen colours. Either follow the photograph on page 85 or use your own colour combinations, paying special attention to the cakes on the counter. Note how some of the plates are also painted to form a colourful backdrop for the cakes.

5 The area beneath the counter is painted to resemble stonework. When the the pale terracotta wash is dry, change to your fine brush and paint the random details of the stonework in a range of pale greys and browns.

6 The two figures behind the counter are also painted, using dark green for the girl's top and Winsor blue for the shopkeeper's pinafore. When the background colour is dry, paint in a pattern of daisies on the pinafore, using white gouache paint for the petals and yellow watercolour for the centres. To finish, apply a warm blush over the face and hands of both figures, using a deeper shade for the rosy cheeks.

Stitching

7 When the painted areas are dry, you can start to apply the stitched details. The shopkeeper's shirt is decorated with French knots using one strand of pale blue Cotton Pearl, while her pinafore is finished with rows of running stitch using a single strand of matching thread to suggest pleats in the fabric. The little girl's green top is decorated with seed stitch in cream thread. The faces of the little girl and the shopkeeper are embroidered with great care using one strand of pink Stranded Embroidery Floss. Their hair is stitched in straight stitch, using three strands of grey or beige Stranded Embroidery Floss.

8 The shopkeeper's body and face are padded in the trapunto technique to give them increased prominence. Cut a piece of closely-woven cotton fabric to back your selected areas and follow the instructions for trapunto on page 28. Highlight the lady's chin and arm by working through the padding with small running stitches. The small girl is left unpadded because she is in the background.

9 The mouthwatering display of cakes on the counter is fun to do and involves a variety of stitches. Start on the right of the display with the painted cake stand. First couch the plates with silver Metallic Cotton Pearl thread, then work the individual cakes. The round cakes on the top tier are decorated with miniature sequins and small glass beads. The cakes on the bottom tier are cut from small squares of peach-coloured felt, couched down with cream chenille thread to suggest fresh cream. Red beads are stitched in the centre of each cake to look like cherries.

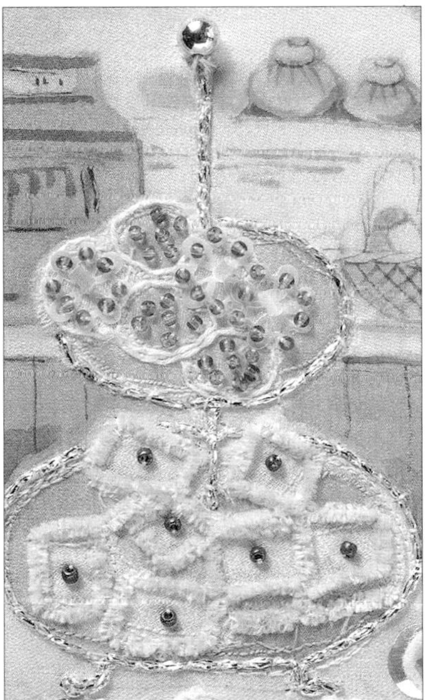

10 The tray in front of the cake stand is also couched in silver Metallic Cotton Pearl thread. It contains six chocolate eclairs, made from oval brown beads, couched around the outside with white chenille thread to resemble fresh cream.

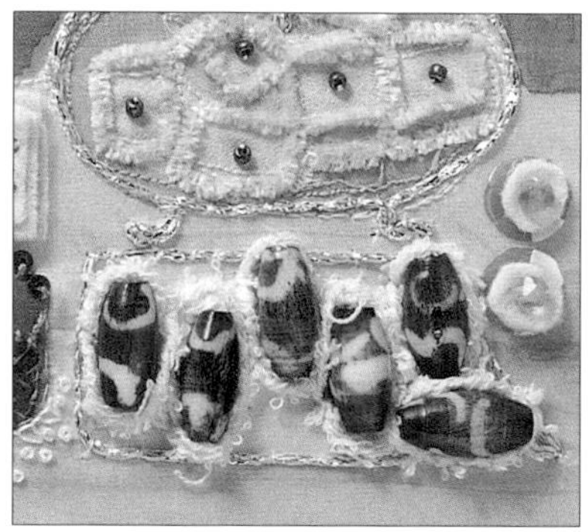

11 Next, embroider the two cherry cakes, which have been painted chocolate brown. Start with the white doily in closed buttonhole stitch and French knots, or couch with silver thread as before, using Cotton Pearl thread. Work the sides of the cake in pale pink seed stitch in Stranded Embroidery Floss. Couch the top edge of the cake in pale pink, and finish with a scattering of red glass bead cherries over the surface.

12 Behind the large chocolate cherry cake are individual cream slices, cut from rectangles of pale orange and white felt and finished with green and blue glass beads to resemble icing. Cut the individual fruit pies in the foreground from circles of felt, in the same manner, and attach them with straight stitches in matching thread. Also make up the iced bakewell tarts on the left-hand side of the counter, this time from circles of white felt, finished with red sequins.

13 The centrepiece is the magnificent pink cake, which is cut from a circle of sugar pink felt, couched around the sides with white chenille thread to look like fresh cream. White chenille straight stitches create a pattern on the top, with a pearl bead at the centre. Pad in the trapunto technique, following the instructions on page 28. Make up the second pink cake on the left-hand side using the same technique, substituting cream chenille thread for the white. No padding is required. When the cakes are complete, stitch the front edge of the counter with three rows of couching in green Stranded Embroidery Floss.

14 The shopkeeper is holding a box of goodies, made from unusual flat beads secured with small yellow or green glass beads. The square box is cut from narrow cream ribbon, which is mitred at the corners and stitched invisibly in position.

15 The final stage is to work the boy and girl in the foreground. First make a template of each child's head and neck from cardboard and use to cut one of each shape from skin-coloured silk, making the silk 6 mm (¼ in) larger all round than the template. Make up the children's heads, following the instructions on page 29, and stitch down securely on the silk with invisible stitches in matching thread.

16 The boy's spiky hair is worked in straight stitch using dark brown and beige Cotton Pearl. The girl's hair is worked in golden yellow Cotton Pearl, following the instructions for stitching and plaiting hair on page 31.

17 The children's bodies are created from three layers of felt each, following the instructions for stumpwork on page 29. The children's clothes are worked in detached buttonhole stitch (see page 44) worked horizontally. Use white Cotton Pearl for the girl's blouse and medium blue for the boy's shirt; leave the sleeves open until you have finished the arms. The boy's shorts are worked in deep purple Cotton Pearl, while the girl's skirt is in green and yellow stripes. Finish with the girl's pinafore straps, created in buttonhole stitch over three lengths of stranded thread. Make up four arms (see page 31) and work the fingers in straight stitch, using skin-coloured thread. Place the arms over the stitched body and tuck them under the open sleeve. Secure the arms to the silk background with invisible stitches and close the sleeve.

TEXTURAL DETAILS

Note how the shopkeeper is padded in the trapunto technique to make her stand out. Her facial features are embroidered with great care and attention to detail.

By the Fire

This intricate design incorporates many different variations of detached buttonhole stitch. The fireplace features a grate made of wire wrapped in grey thread and a realistic fire, which sparkles with sequins and brightly coloured bullion knots. A tabby cat completes the scene.

Materials

- Off-white pure silk backed with soft butter muslin (cheesecloth), 35 x 40 cm (14 x 15 in)
- Embroidery frame, 30 x 34 cm (12 x 13 in)
- Stapler
- Drawing paper
- Soft pencil
- Thin cardboard (postcard weight)
- Tailor's chalk
- Artist's brushes, nos. 10 and 12
- Watercolour paints: Winsor blue, Winsor yellow and permanent rose
- Needle
- Striped satin fabric for the rug
- A little cream silk for the clockface
- A little pink suede for the clock frame and slippers
- PVA glue
- Oval gold beads for the pendulums
- Red velvet ribbon for the mantlepiece runner
- Red, pink and orange sequins
- A few florist's medium-gauge stub wires
- Narrow gold ribbon for the fender
- Round gold beads for the fender
- Silver kid for the candlestick
- Felt in mustard yellow and purple for padding the person, the chair and the cat
- Florist's fine-gauge wire or fuse wire
- Yellow leather for the book
- DMC Metallic Embroidery Floss in gold (5282)
- DMC Metallic Cotton Pearl in gold (5282)
- DMC Cotton Pearl in grey (413)
- DMC Special Embroidery Cotton in the following colours:

  Blues/purples: 796, 798, 3325, 553, 554

  Green: 703

  White/cream: B5200, Ecru

  Red/pink: 321, 819
- DMC Stranded Embroidery Floss in the following colours:

  Yellow/orange: 973, 970

  Brown: 3860

  Greys: 762, 318, 414, 413

STITCHES

1 Straight stitch
2 Detached buttonhole stitch
3 Herringbone stitch
4 Satin stitch
5 Cretan stitch
6 Running stitch
7 Couching
8 Bullion knot
9 Buttonhole filling stitch
10 Threaded running stitch
11 French knots
12 Seed stitch

Preparation

1 Staple the silk and muslin (cheesecloth) to the wooden frame, keeping the grain of the fabric straight as it is stretched taut (see page 23).

2 Sketch your basic design on to a piece of drawing paper the same size as the inner edge of your frame, using the stitch diagram opposite as a guide. Make a full-size template of the armchair, the fireplace and the clock from cardboard, and arrange the shapes on the silk. Lightly draw around the templates with a soft pencil or tailor's chalk. Mark the position of the grate and the kettle in the fireplace. Then draw in the pattern of the stonework on either side of the chimney.

3 You are now ready to apply the watercolour paint. Take your smallest paintbrush and carefully draw in the vertical lines of the wallpaper in pale blue paint. Next, paint the detail of the cast-iron fireplace in shades of grey, following the photograph. Add a few red embers in the hearth, with a small brush. For further information on mixing watercolours, see page 26.

Stitching

4 The wallpaper is worked in running stitch using a single strand of pale mauve Special Embroidery Cotton. Start at the top of the picture and follow the wavy lines of the watercolour, finishing level with the floor.

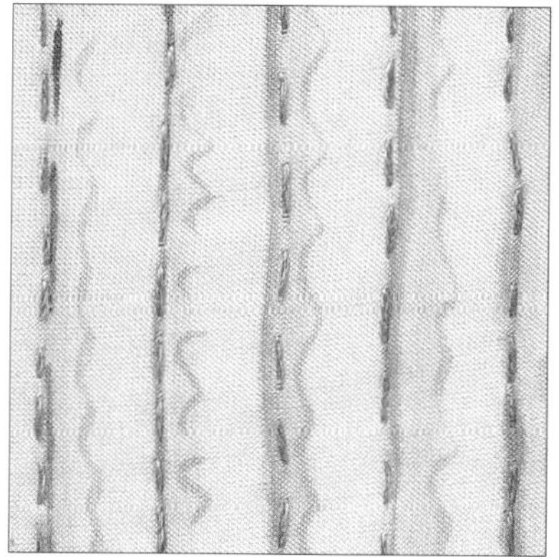

5 Choose a piece of striped fabric for the rug and cut it to size. Stitch down invisibly on the silk background, then embroider the fringes at either end in straight stitch, using purple Special Embroidery Cotton.

6 The clockface is made from silk fabric with a pink suede border. Use the template of the clock cut in Step 2 to draw an outline of the shape on to cream silk. Before you cut out the shape, embroider the time and numerals in straight stitch using one strand of gold Metallic Embroidery Floss. Assemble the clockface, then cut a circular frame of pink suede to fit over the clock-face, and stitch invisibly in place. Position the clock on the wall and secure with invisible stitches. Couch the inner and outer edges of the clock frame with gold Metallic Cotton Pearl and create a bow at the top. Finish with two chains, couched down in the same way. Attach an oval gold bead at the base of each chain.

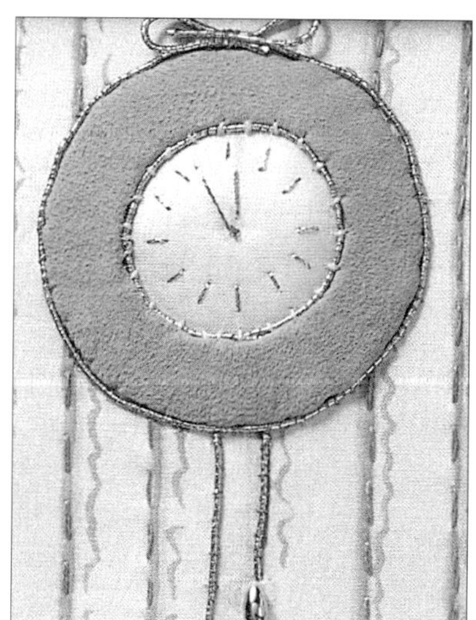

7 The mantlepiece is created from red velvet ribbon. Cut two pieces of ribbon the same length as the mantlepiece. Secure them to the silk with invisible stitches. Create a fringed edging in detached buttonhole stitch, using matching deep red Special Embroidery Cotton. Decorate with red sequins at each point.

8 Cut four pieces of florist's stub wire for the grate and wrap them tightly with grey thread (see page 30). Bend the wires slightly to create a curved shape and fix in place on the embroidery. First use the ends of the wire to pierce the silk, then secure on the back with a few stitches. Work the rest of the basket in buttonhole filling stitch and herringbone stitch, in matching grey Cotton Pearl. You can now embroider the stonework on either side of the chimney in shades of grey and mauve, using buttonhole filling stitches for a textured effect. Use dark brown for the kettle.

9 The fire's flames are a very decorative feature, using red, pink and orange sequins to shine alongside the gold stitchery and bullion knots in similar colours. Note how a few gold bullion knots sparkle among the ashes beneath the grate.

10 The brass fender is created from a piece of narrow gold ribbon, which is couched in place with matching gold thread. Round gold beads decorate the top of the fender.

11 You can now introduce some ornaments on the mantlepiece. The two painted silk plates are mounted on cardboard in the same way as the clockface. The lids of the jars and the candlestick are cut from silver kid and secured with invisible stitches. The candle is created from a bullion knot using green Special Embroidery Cotton.

12 The next stage is to assemble the armchair. Use your template to cut three shapes from felt, making one 3 mm (1/8 in) smaller all round than the other. Tack (baste) the shapes together, following the instructions for stumpwork on page 29, and stitch down on the silk background. Decorate the back of the chair with detached buttonhole stitch worked vertically in mid-blue Special Embroidery Cotton. Work the side of the chair in a deeper shade of blue using horizontal buttonhole filling stitch with pink French knots for decoration. Finish with two chair legs,

cut from purple felt and stitched in place. Make up the stool from felt in the same way as the chair, and embroider in deep purple detached buttonhole stitch using Special Embroidery Cotton. Work a blue band around the middle of the stool in straight stitch.

13 Make up the person's arms and legs from felt, following the instructions for stumpwork on page 29. Decorate with detached buttonhole stitch, using blue and cream Special Embroidery Cotton for the striped trousers and green for the arm. The hand is made by wrapping short lengths of fine-gauge florist's wire with one strand of pink Special Embroidery Cotton (see page 30). The socks are worked in satin stitch using green cotton. The slippers are cut from pink suede and secured with tiny stitches in matching thread. The book is cut from yellow leather, with individual paper pages glued inside. Place the book in the hand and glue into place with PVA glue. The pipe is worked in raised satin stitch in dark brown Stranded Embroidery Floss – note the puff of smoke in threaded running stitch.

14 The final stage is to embroider the tabby cat on the rug. Make up a felt stumpwork cat (see page 29) and secure on the rug with invisible stitches. Work the stripes on the fur in Cretan stitch using pale cream Special Embroidery Cotton. Finish with the emerald green eyes, created in straight stitch, and a little pink nose.

Textural effects

The fireplace incorporates a variety of stitches and detailed painting to capture the intricate pattern of the cast-iron grate and the ornate stone surround.

Formal Garden

My husband is a keen gardener and it seemed appropriate to record our formal garden, with its stone fountain and classical flower urns. The result is a highly textured thread painting, with an abundance of colour and lots of different stitches.

Materials

- Cream pure silk backed with soft butter muslin (cheesecloth), 45 x 38 cm (18 x 14 in)
- Embroidery frame, 40 x 32 cm (16 x 12 in)
- Stapler
- Drawing paper
- Soft pencil
- Artist's brushes, nos. 10 and 12
- Watercolour paints: Winsor blue, Winsor yellow and permanent rose
- A few florist's medium-gauge stub wires
- Needle
- Moss-green felt
- Moss-green chenille thread
- Closely-woven cotton fabric for backing the trapunto areas
- White embroidery silk or fine crochet cotton
- A little cotton wadding (batting)
- DMC Metallic Embroidery Floss in silver (5283)
- DMC Stranded Embroidery Floss in the following colours:

  BEIGES/BROWNS: 3033, 3032, 644, 869

  PINKS: 778, 3689, 3688

  CREAMS/YELLOW: 3078, 3823, 725

  GREENS: 369, 936, 890, 472

  PURPLES/BLUES: 554, 553, 552, 327, 3753, 809

  WHITE: B5200

Kit 93

STITCHES

1 Buttonhole filling stitch

2 French knot

3 Eyelet stitch

4 Cretan stitch

5 Bullion rose knot

6 Detached chain stitch

7 Satin stitch with French knots in the centre

8 Couching

9 Running stitch

10 Seed stitch

Preparation

1 Staple the silk and muslin (cheesecloth) to the wooden frame, keeping the grain of the fabric straight as it is stretched taut (see page 23).

2 Sketch your basic design on to a piece of drawing paper the same size as the inner edge of your frame, using the stitch diagram opposite as a guide. I included the urn, the fountain, the outline of the path and the horizon. Transfer the design on to your silk using one of the methods described on page 25.

3 You are now ready to apply the watercolour paint. I chose a dark, contrasting background behind the splashing fountain and rose arch, to display them to advantage. Use your largest paintbrush, fully loaded with Winsor blue, and start to wash in the sky area. Next, introduce a hazy dark green along the horizon line, followed by a soft grey-green on either side of the path. Now change to a smaller paintbrush in order to outline the base of the fountain, the path and the urn. Finally, introduce a little detail on the path and urn using yellow and green watercolour to indicate the stonework and shadows. For further information on mixing watercolours, see page 26.

4 When the background colours are dry, paint in the small and distant trees on the horizon and the flowerbeds beneath them using a brush with a fine tip. Try to make the images appear vague and blurred, to introduce a sense of perspective.

Stitching

5 The first stage is to make the rose arch. This is cut from three pieces of florist's stub wire, which are wrapped tightly with white embroidery silk or fine crochet cotton (see page 30) and then bent into arch shapes. The twisted wisteria vines are created in the same way, but green and brown thread are used in place of the white. After wrapping the wires with thread, bend them into shape before fastening them in place on the silk using invisible stitches. Couch the horizontal bars of the arch using two strands of white thread. You can now introduce the leaves and flowers of the wisteria. For variety, I cut some leaves from moss-green felt and stitched the rest in chenille thread using French knots. The wisteria flowers are embroidered in shades of mauve and purple using buttonhole filling stitch and two strands of thread.

6 The next step is to embroider the roses on the right-hand side of the arch. These are worked in two shades of pink, using small French knots for the buds and large bullion knots for the flowers. The rose leaves are detached chain stitch in two shades of green.

7 The flower border on the left-hand side of the path is worked in pretty pastel shades. Start by embroidering the palest flowers in the foreground, using French knots in white, pink and green thread. Work the leaves in shades of green, using detached chain loops. Next, create the daisy-like flowers using individual eyelet stitches in white or yellow. Finish with the pink, blue and mauve flowers at the foot of the fountain, using French knots for the flowers and detached chain loops for the leaves.

8 The urn is brimming with colour and interest and for this I chose a wide variety of stitches and colours. Start by working the flowers in your chosen colours, referring to the stitch diagram on page 98, then work the relief pattern on the urn in running stitch using one strand of beige thread.

9 You can now work the pattern on the path in running stitch and seed stitch using one strand of thread in shades of beige. Note how the stitching is concentrated along the right-hand side of the path to suggest shadows.

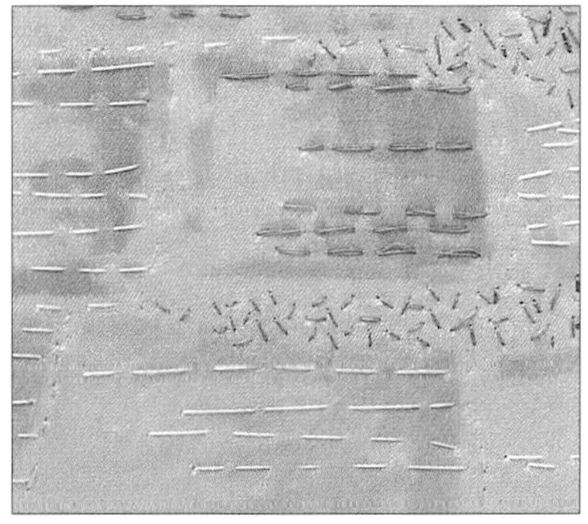

10 The water spray of the fountain is brought to life with tiny running stitches in silver Metallic Embroidery thread, using one strand only.

11 The base of the fountain, the urn filled with embroidered flowers and part of the flower border on the left-hand side, are padded in the trapunto technique to give them increased prominence. Cut a piece of cotton fabric large enough to cover the entire area to be padded, and follow the instructions for trapunto on page 28.

12 The fabric-covered mount is decorated using the 'English' method of quilting to indicate stonework. For information on quilting the mount, see page 33.

PERSPECTIVE

Note how the groups of flowers in the left-hand border become smaller as they drift into the distance, leading your eye towards the focal point of the fountain.

The Welsh Dresser

For this raised embroidery, I chose a green silk background to offset the objects on display. These include a cactus, a vase of irises and a bowl of fruit. The design for the blue-and-white plate was based on a favourite item on my dresser at home.

Materials

- Green silk backed with fine cotton sheeting, 45 x 38 cm (18 x 14 in)
- Embroidery frame, 40 x 32 cm (16 x 12 in)
- Stapler
- Drawing paper
- Soft pencil
- Thin and thick cardboard
- Tailor's chalk
- Ruler
- Needle
- White cotton lawn fabric
- White scalloped lace edging, 10 mm (½ in) wide
- Narrow white lace ribbon, 5 mm (¼ in) wide
- A little white silk satin for the large plate
- Miniature plastic bottles
- Wooden beads or cotton moulds in assorted shapes and sizes, small dark red beads
- Embroidery raffia
- PVA glue
- A few florist's medium- and fine-gauge stub wires
- 2 m (2 yd) florist's fine-gauge wire or fuse wire
- DMC Cotton Pearl in the following colours:
  Greens: 989, 3348, 367
  Blues: 809, 828
  Reds: 3328, 3685
  Orange/yellow: 742, 445
  White/beiges: B5200, 945, 3823
- DMC Stranded Embroidery Floss in the following colours:
  Blues/purple: 800, 809, 3042
  White: B5200

Kit 93

STITCHES

1 Running stitch
2 Threaded running stitch
3 Treble Brussels stitch
4 Satin stitch
5 Open loop stitch
6 Buttonhole stitch
7 Straight stitch
8 Closed buttonhole stitch
9 Detached buttonhole stitch
10 Treble Brussels stitch, with French knot at each opening
11 Looped ring picot
12 Couching
13 Couronne loop
14 Buttonhole filling stitch

Preparation

1 Staple the silk and cotton to the wooden frame, keeping the grain of the fabric straight as it is stretched taut (see page 23).

2 Sketch your basic design on to a piece of drawing paper the same size as the inner edge of your frame, using the stitch diagram on page 104 as a guide. Transfer the outline of the dresser on to the silk using tailor's chalk. Then use a ruler to mark the position of the shelves and drawers, and the vertical lines on the back of the dresser. Make a full-size template of the large plate from thin cardboard.

Stitching

3 First, embroider the wooden panels on the back of the dresser. Thread your needle with one strand of white Stranded Embroidery Floss and follow the chalk lines using a neat running stitch. Create a second, wavy line in threaded running stitch, again using one strand of thread.

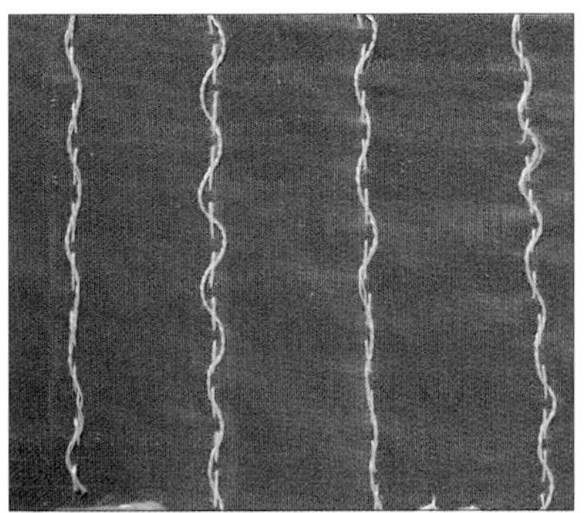

4 The next step is to make the shelves. Measure the width of your dresser and cut two pieces of thick cardboard the same width, making them 1.5 cm (½ in) deep. Cut two strips of cotton lawn 4 cm (1½ in) wide and slightly longer than your pieces of cardboard. Wrap the fabric around the cardboard to enclose it and secure along one edge with stitches. Fold in the ends to neaten them and secure with stitches. Stitch a piece of scalloped lace edging along the front edge of each piece of covered card. Stitch the shelves on to the silk background. Cut three pieces of narrow ribbon the same length as the shelves, and stitch one under each shelf and the third close to the top of the dresser.

5 Work the two drawers in lace filling stitch, using white Cotton Pearl thread. Cut two pieces of narrow ribbon to fit around the drawers and stitch down with invisible stitches, mitring the corners neatly. Choose two beads for the drawer handles and stitch to the centre of each drawer.

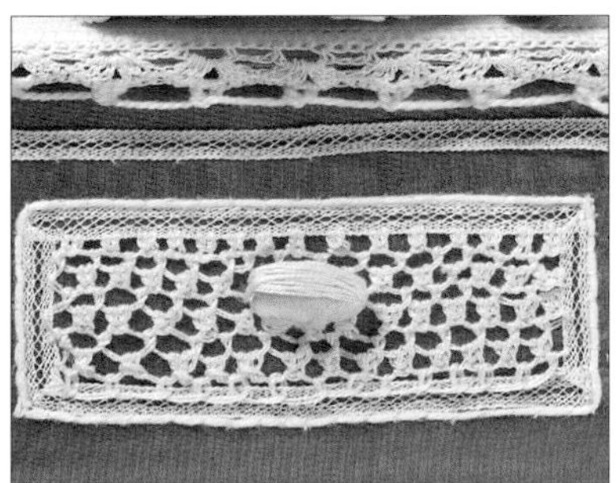

6 The large plate is made from white silk satin fabric, decorated with blue stitching. Cut a rectangle of white silk slightly larger than your cardboard template, then draw around the template on to the silk. Before you cut out the shape, it is a good idea to embroider or paint the pattern in your chosen colours. I chose to embroider the plate in blue and purple Stranded Embroidery Floss using one strand of thread. My design incorporates satin stitch, open loop stitch, buttonhole stitch and straight stitch. Rows of running stitch and closed buttonhole stitch surround the inner edge. When the pattern is complete, cut out and mount the embroidered silk on the cardboard template. Position the plate on the dresser and glue into place.

7 The collection of pots on the shelves is quite unique. The vase, flowerpot and jug are created from individual plastic bottles – the type that are used for perfume samples – which are cut in half to form a cross-section and wrapped with Cotton Pearl thread to anchor the decorative stitching. First choose a plastic bottle the right size, cut it in half lengthways, then bind it tightly with your chosen thread – I used white Cotton Pearl for the flower vase and pale blue for the flowerpot and jug. When the plastic is fully covered with thread, work the decorative areas in a deeper or contrasting colour using buttonhole filling stitch. The handle of the jug is created from a short length of florist's stub wire, wrapped tightly with matching thread and bent into a curved shape before being stitched to the side of the jug.

8 The fruit basket is made from plaited raffia. Take three pieces of raffia and one piece of fine wire, approximately 1 m (3 ft) in length, and plait them together to form a long piece of rope. Bend the resulting rope into a basket shape and stitch together at intervals to secure the individual layers. Trim away any excess raffia, then finish with a handle created from raffia in the same way.

9 The basket contains a variety of different coloured fruits. Use wooden beads or cotton moulds as a base for the fruit – oval beads for lemons and so on – and decorate them with detached buttonhole stitch, using Cotton Pearl thread. When the stitched areas are complete, decorate the fruits with leaves or stems, created by wrapping florist's medium-gauge stub wire with beige or green thread (see page 30).

10 The cactus is created from oval beads covered with detached buttonhole stitch in two colours. Prepare the beads in the same way as the coloured fruits, then stitch them together at intervals to resemble a cactus plant. Glue the cactus into the flowerpot, adding a few dark red beads at the base to suggest buds.

11 The yellow and white irises are created from fine florist's wire, which is bent into shape before being bound with thread and finished with embroidery (see page 30).

12 The only remaining item on the dresser is the small round plate. This is stitched directly onto the silk background, using buttonhole filling stitch worked from a central point in blue and white Cotton Pearl to resemble a doily.

13 When you are happy with your collection of objects, spend a little time positioning them on the shelves to make a pleasing arrangement, before glueing them invisibly on to the silk background.

14 The final stage is to make the dresser top. Start by creating the scalloped edge at the top of the dresser from narrow ribbon, decorated along the top edge with looped picot stitch. Next work the deep band of lace in the centre using treble Brussels stitch with French knots in each opening. Finish with the couronne loops.

VASE OF IRISES

The miniature iris flowers are created from fine florist's wire, which is bound with Cotton Pearl thread and then decorated with detached buttonhole stitch. The leaves are a thicker stub wire wrapped in the same thread.

Playing the Violin

I made this thread painting for my granddaughter, Charlotte, whose favourite pastime is playing her violin. The girl is created using the traditional method of stumpwork, with special attention paid to her hands. The violin is cut from fine leather, while the shoes are made from tiny pieces of felt.

Materials

- Cream pure silk fabric backed with soft butter muslin (cheesecloth), 35 x 40 cm (14 x 15 in)
- Embroidery frame, 30 x 34 cm (12 x 13 in)
- Stapler
- Soft pencil
- Drawing paper
- Artist's brushes, nos. 10 and 12
- Watercolour paints: Winsor blue, Winsor yellow and permanent rose
- Needle
- Flesh-coloured felt for the girl's dress and legs
- Flesh-coloured silk satin for the girl's face
- Pink suede for the girl's shoes
- Two crystal beads
- Florist's fine-gauge wire or fuse wire for the girl's fingers and the violin bow
- Brown leather for the violin
- Black felt-tip pen
- PVA glue
- DMC Stranded Embroidery Floss in the following colours:
  Blue/purple: 3325, 552
  Yellow/white: 3822, B5200
  Pinks: 606, 603
  Greens: 772, 3348, 368
  Browns/black: 840, 842, 898, 310
- DMC Cotton Pearl in the following colours:
  Pinks: 818, 3326

Kit 94

STITCHES

1 Closed buttonhole stitch
2 French knot
3 Seed stitch
4 Open buttonhole stitch
5 Running stitch
6 Herringbone stitch
7 Open loop stitch
8 Bullion knot
9 Detached chain stitch
10 Straight stitch
11 Satin stitch
12 Detached buttonhole stitch
13 Looped ring picot

Preparation

1 Staple the silk and muslin (cheesecloth) to the wooden frame, keeping the grain of the fabric straight as it is stretched taut (see page 23).

2 Sketch the basic outline of the girl, rug, curtain and wallpaper on to a piece of drawing paper the same size as the inner edge of your frame. Make a paper template of each motif by cutting out the shapes individually. Group the templates on the silk in a pleasing arrangement and lightly draw around them with a pencil.

3 You are now ready to apply the watercolour paint. Start by painting a faint wash over the back wall using a medium brush and pale green, created by mix ing Winsor blue and Winsor yellow together. When the wall is dry, paint the floor area with a pale blue wash. For further information on mixing watercolours, see page 26.

4 You can now introduce the painted details. The striped wallpaper, floral curtain, oval rug, plant pots and fern leaves are all painted with delicate strokes using a brush with a fine tip. Use the photograph as a guide and apply the paint fairly dry to prevent the colours from running into the fabric.

Stitching

5 Begin by working the ruffled edge of the curtain in closed buttonhole stitch, using two strands of pale blue Stranded Embroidery Floss. Next stitch the French knots on the curtain using two strands of yellow. Finish with the seed stitches using one strand of purple. To suggest the folds of the drapes, work diagonal rows of running stitch across the curtain in matching thread.

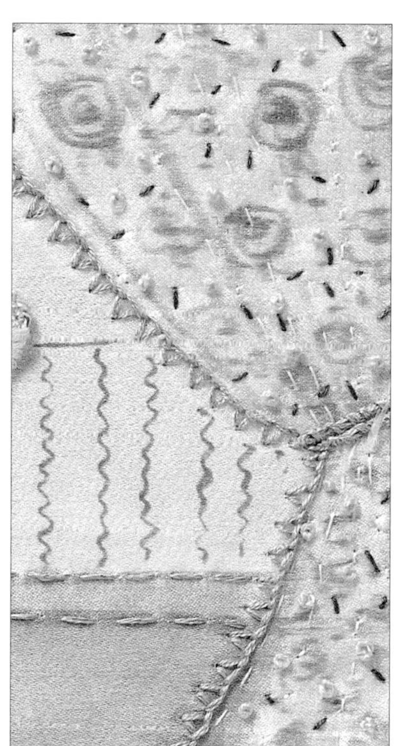

6 When the curtain is complete, highlight the skirting board and dado rail with parallel rows of running stitch, using two strands of pale pink Stranded Embroidery Floss.

7 The rug is stitched in shades of pink, mauve, green and yellow, using two or three strands of Stranded Embroidery Floss. Start in the centre of the rug with a scattering of purple seed stitches. Work the first herringbone border in fuchsia pink, then add a second border close to the first in pale green, followed by a row of purple running stitch. Finish with the outer fringe, worked in open buttonhole stitch using pale pink thread.

8 The fern is worked in open loop stitch in an irregular pattern. Follow the painted lines, using two strands of medium and pale green Stranded Embroidery Floss. You can now work the pink roses in bullion knots, using two strands of thread. Finish with the clusters of rose leaves in detached chain stitch using two strands of green.

9 Cut away the head of your paper template of the girl, to leave the dress and arms. Draw around the template on to a piece of flesh-coloured felt and cut out the shape. Cut a second piece of felt the same shape as the first, making it slightly smaller all round. Assemble the dress from felt, following the instructions for stumpwork on page 29, and stitch it down invisibly on the silk background fabric. Cut a small piece of felt to form the arm holding the bow (a small semi-circle should be sufficient) and stitch invisibly on to the felt dress to make it protrude slightly.

10 The girl's face is created using the soft-sculpture technique. First cut an oval shape from flesh-coloured silk, slightly larger all round than the girl's face. Assemble the face, following the instructions for soft sculpture on page 29, and stitch down securely on to the silk with invisible stitches. Work the facial features in tiny stitches, using one strand of medium brown, then work the hair in straight stitch using two strands of medium and light brown Stranded Embroidery Floss.

11 The dress is worked in two shades of pink Cotton Pearl, using a simple version of needlelace detached buttonhole stitch. Start at the neckline of the dress with a foundation row of deep pink detached buttonhole stitch, working from left to right. Embroider three rows of deep pink, then introduce the pale shade. Use the pale pink thread to buttonhole stitch into each loop of the previous row, from right to left. The stitch is caught into the felt at the beginning and end of each row only – don't pierce the silk fabric at any other point. Stitch alternate rows of deep and light pink, increasing the width of each row by adding an extra stitch at either end. When the dress is complete, embroider a narrow belt around the girl's waist using straight stitch and purple Stranded Embroidery Floss. To finish, decorate the hem of the skirt with two rows of looped ring picot to give a scalloped edge.

12 The legs are made from small rectangles of flesh-coloured felt. Cut out two rectangles, then roll them up tightly to form two tubes and secure the overlapping edges with running stitches. Tuck the legs underneath the skirt, placing the overlapping edges at the back to hide the join. Stitch in place with invisible stitch, then work the socks using satin stitch in white thread. Cut out two small shoes from pink suede and secure in place with tiny stitches in matching thread. Finish with a crystal bead on the front of each shoe to suggest a buckle.

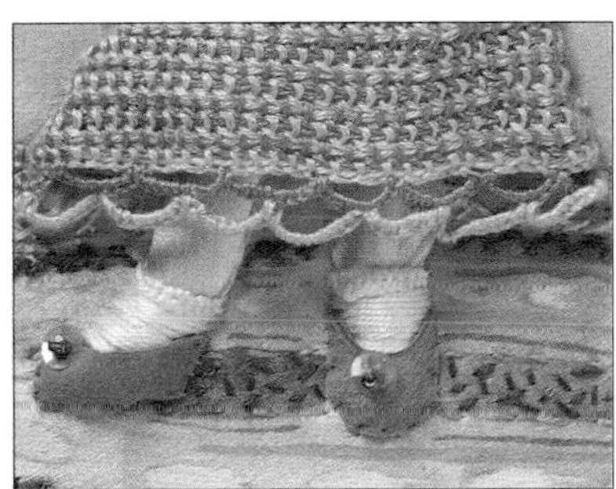

13 The hands need to be fashioned with special attention, since they are very much a feature of this little study. Start by wrapping the fine wire with one strand of pale pink Stranded Embroidery Floss, then follow the instructions for making hands on page 30. Stitch the hands on to the background fabric and carefully bend them into shape.

14 Make a template for the violin from paper and use it to cut a shape from fine leather. Draw in the details on the leather violin with a black felt-tip pen and glue into place. Create the bow from wire wrapped in dark brown Stranded Embroidery Floss, and glue into position. To finish, carefully bend the girl's fingers around the bow and violin.

Composition

It is important to allow plenty of space to accommodate the figure of the child, which is the focus of interest. The background structure should be simple but nicely balanced, to provide a backcloth for the child.

Statue of Pan

This stone statue of Pan is a favourite feature in our garden. Here I have given it increased prominence by silhouetting it against a dark blue and green background underneath a standard rose tree.

Materials

- Cream pure silk backed with soft butter muslin (cheesecloth), 45 x 38 cm (18 x 14 in)
- Embroidery frame, 40 x 32 cm (16 x 12 in)
- Stapler
- Drawing paper
- Soft pencil
- Artist's brushes, nos. 10 and 12
- Watercolour paints: Winsor blue, Winsor yellow and permanent rose
- Needle
- Closely-woven cotton fabric for backing the trapunto areas
- A little cotton wadding (batting)
- DMC Stranded Embroidery Floss in the following colours:

  Purples/blues: 211, 806, 553, 554, 598, 747

  Greens: 772, 3348, 3346, 907, 522, 966, 3345, 368, 320, 989

  Reds/pinks: 304, 3804, 604, 601, 819, 776, 754, 605

  Greys/white: 645, 644, B5200

  Creams/yellows: 822, 746, 745, 744, 3822, 3823

  Orange: 722

  Browns/beige: 830, 610, 611, 613

Stitches

1	Padded satin stitch	**5**	Stem stitch	**9**	Running stitch
2	Bullion knot	**6**	Detached chain stitch	**10**	Cretan stitch
3	French knot	**7**	Seed stitch	**11**	Eyelet stitch
4	Couching	**8**	Buttonhole stitch	**12**	Vertical Cretan stitch

Preparation

1 Staple the silk and muslin (cheesecloth) to the wooden frame, keeping the grain of the fabric straight as it is stretched taut (see page 23).

2 Sketch your basic design on to a piece of drawing paper the same size as the inner edge of your frame, using the stitch diagram opposite as a guide. I included the outline of the pond, the statue and the rose tree. When you are happy with the composition, transfer your design on to the silk using one of the methods described on page 25.

3 You are now ready to apply the watercolour paint. Use your largest brush to paint the area behind the statue in a variety of different glowing colours, allowing them to blend together to provide a backcloth for the figure of Pan. When you are happy with the background, paint in the area around the

pond in shades of green. Now change to a smaller brush and paint the tree on the horizon and the bushes, making them appear vague and blurred to introduce a feeling of perspective. For further information on mixing watercolours, see page 26.

4 The water is painted in two shades of blue. Small areas of cream silk are left free of colour to suggest sunlight on the water. The shadows on the stonework are painted a light beige colour.

Stitching

5 This piece uses a variety of stitches to capture the exquisite textures of the flowers. Working from right to left, start by embroidering the border in the foreground using one or two strands of thread. The geraniums in the right-hand corner consist of tiny clusters of French knots, with eyelet stitch for the leaves. The orange roses are stitched in buttonhole stitch with clusters of French knots at the centre.

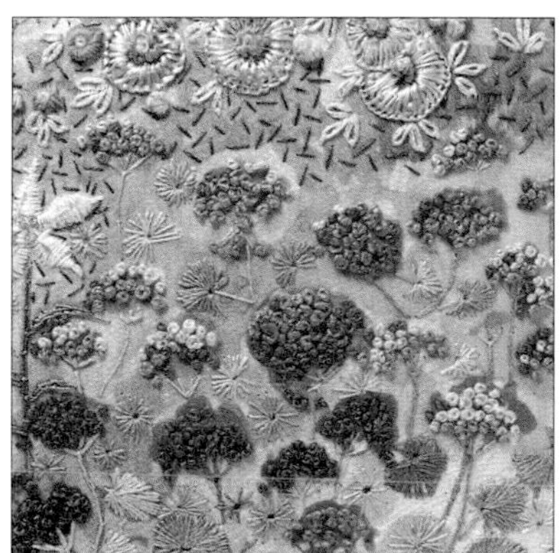

6 The elegant lilies are embroidered in padded satin stitch, using white thread for the flowers and shades of green for the stem-stitched leaves.

7 The purple and mauve irises are embroidered in a variety of stitches, with couching for the leaves. When you are happy with the depth of colour in the flower borders, introduce a little texture around some of the flowers with irregular seed stitch.

8 The arching trunk of the rose tree is embroidered in stem stitch using three shades of brown. Group the roses along the branches, using golden yellow bullion knots in different sizes to represent buds and flowers. Finish with a background of leaves in detached chain stitch using dark and medium green to contrast with the flowers.

9 The stone statue of Pan is only lightly stitched to contrast with the highly textured background. Start by outlining the shape of the statue with an even running stitch in cream embroidery thread, then introduce a series of shadows down the right-hand side in shades of beige and grey. Use the same colours to highlight the cobbles around the pond.

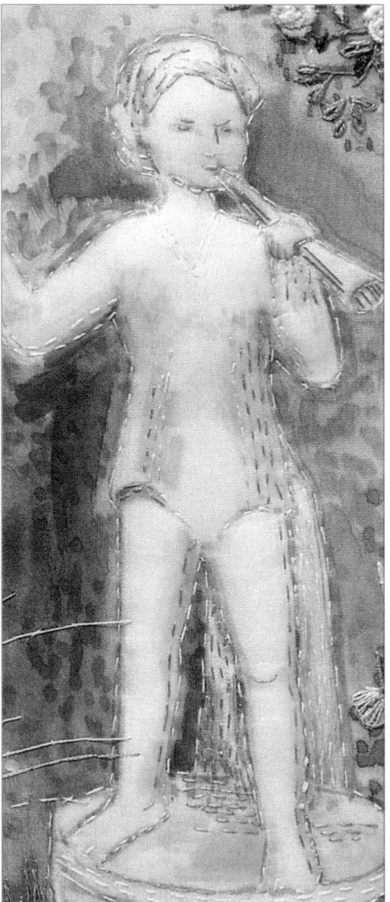

10 The next stage is to work the pond. Start by highlighting the ripples on the pond using horizontal Cretan stitch in shades of blue and purple. Use a single strand of light or dark green thread to couch the tall bullrush stems, and zigzag stitch to suggest shadows in the water. Finally, work the bullrush seedheads in bullion knots, using two strands of dark brown thread.

11 The statue, rose tree, flower border and front edge of the pond are padded in the trapunto technique to give them increased prominence. Back the entire area with closely-woven cotton fabric, then follow the instructions for trapunto on page 28.

12 The final stage is to make the mount, which is decorated with small running stitches, using the 'English' method of quilting (see page 33), in shades of beige and cream, to resemble stonework.

STITCHING

The wealth of summer flowers in the foreground provides a wonderful opportunity for experimenting with different stitches.

Golden Angel

My inspiration for this thread painting came from an ancient stone carving of an angel in a local churchyard. I had to simplify the image slightly before transferring it to silk, and chose a combination of gold paint, stitching and padding to create a highly embossed effect.

STITCHES

1 Couching
2 Open loop stitch
3 Open buttonhole stitch
4 Fly stitch
5 Straight stitch
6 Buttonhole filling stitch
7 Star stitch
8 Threaded running stitch

Materials

- Cream pure silk fabric backed with soft butter muslin (cheesecloth), 35 x 40 cm (14 x 15 in)
- Embroidery frame, 30 x 34 cm (12 x 13 in)
- Stapler
- Soft pencil
- Gold gouache paint
- Watercolour paints: Winsor blue, Winsor yellow and permanent rose
- Artist's brushes, nos. 10 and 12
- Needle
- Closely-woven cotton fabric for backing the trapunto areas
- A little cotton wadding (batting)
- DMC Stranded Metallic Floss in gold (5282)
- DMC Stranded Embroidery Floss in the following colours:

  Mauve: 3835

  Yellow: 3821

  Creams: 3866, 3865

Preparation

1 Staple the silk and muslin (cheesecloth) to the wooden frame, keeping the grain of the fabric straight as it is stretched taut (see page 23).

2 Use a pencil to sketch the outline of the angel and the borders on to the silk, using the diagram on page 120 as a guide.

3 Begin painting the linear sections of the pattern using gold gouache paint. Block in the solid areas of gold with a medium brush, then add the detail on the wings and the feathers. Use a small brush to 'spot' paint over the upper area of the silk for further interest.

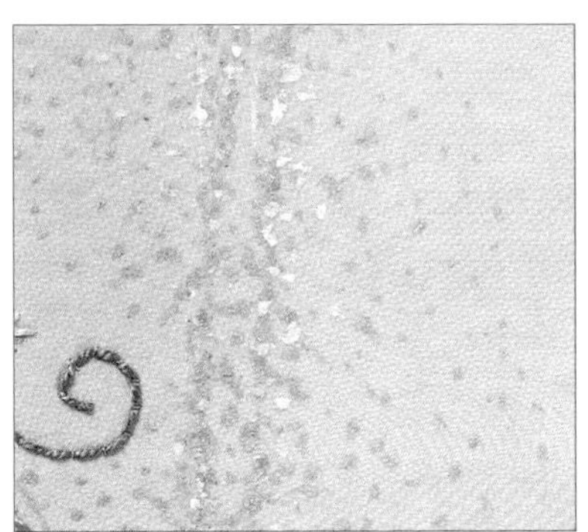

4 Mix up a warm, purple-brown colour by combining your three watercolour paints (see page 26). Paint small areas to create pattern on the wings. Block in and shade the area below the feathers and around the hair. Dapple on the paint to imitate stitching and throw the face and hair into relief. Shade the face very carefully to give an antiqued quality, using a light touch to create a pleasant expression. Add the angel's curls in soft grey and brown tones. For further information on mixing watercolours, see page 26.

Stitching

5 Outline the linear elements of the design with simple rows of couching. The oval inner border that surrounds the angel is couched with six strands of mauve thread, tied down with one strand of metallic thread. Add a row of threaded running stitch in metallic thread around the top mauve border. Use the mauve to create the flourish at the top. Work the gold painted leaves in open loop stitch, using two strands of cream. Finish with an eight-pointed star stitch in the centre, using two strands of metallic gold thread.

6 The outer border that surrounds the angel is couched with six strands of golden yellow thread, tied down with one strand of metallic gold. Use the yellow thread to outline the angel's wings and feathers. Create the scalloped border above the angel's head in fly stitch, using one strand of pale cream thread.

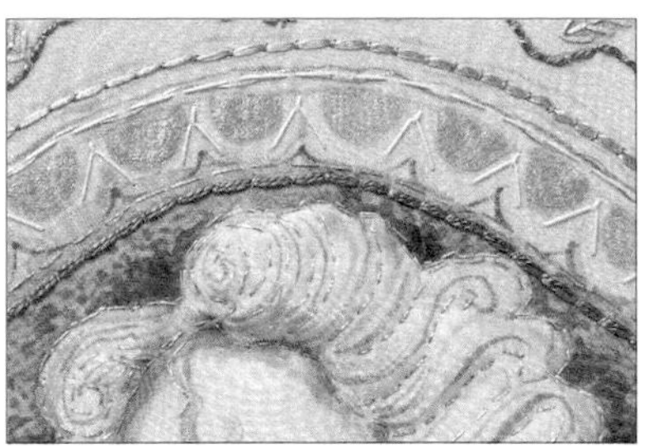

7 You can now add further interest to the painted borders by infilling with open buttonhole stitch. Use two strands of cream to stitch over the golden areas at the base of the picture.

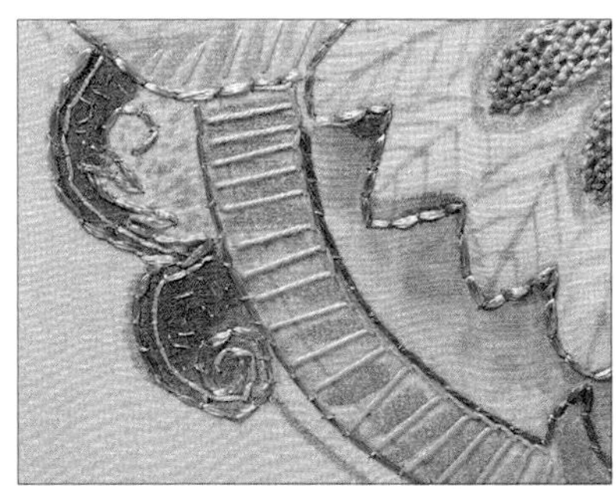

8 The feathered effect on the wings is created with rows of straight stitch in cream, and running stitch in mauve.

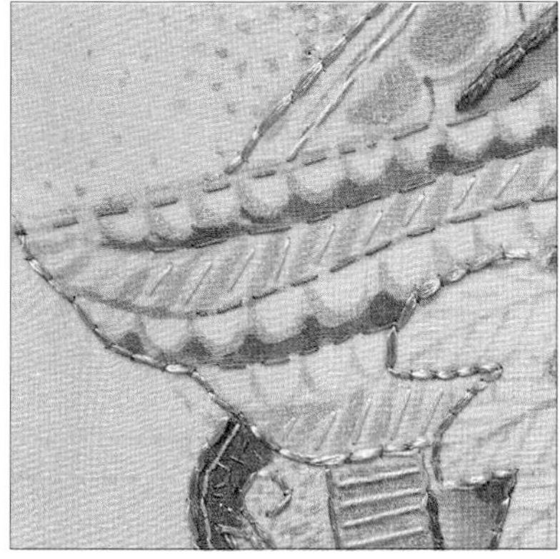

9 The angel's feathered ruffle is stitched using open loop stitch and buttonhole filling stitch to give a highly textured finish. Start by working the feathers directly below the angel's face in open loop stitch, using two strands of metallic gold thread. Then add the second layer of longer feathers in buttonhole filling stitch, using two shades of cream and finishing with mauve at the tips.

10 The face, hair and wings are softly padded in the trapunto technique. Cut a piece of cotton fabric to cover the entire area to be padded and follow the instructions for trapunto on page 28.

11 Embroider the facial features with care, in small straight stitch, using a single strand of cream thread, working through the padding to give a soft, sculpted expression. Indicate the locks of hair with rows of straight stitch to give a quilted appearance, using one strand of gold metallic thread.

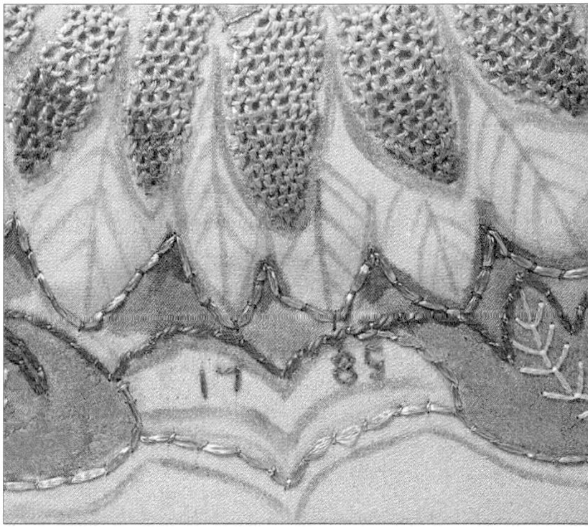

INSPIRATION

The inspiration for this angel design came from a visit to the church of Cley-next-the-Sea, where I found a crumbling stone carving dated 1785.

Index

Acknowledgements

Author's Acknowledgements
My thanks go to my husband, Peter, for so patiently photographing my thread paintings in order for me to introduce them to Collins & Brown.

Also, many thanks to Moya Myerscough for her kindly attention at all times, expertly typing my scribbled words and to Michael Hill of Picture Craft for his encouragement and support.

Publisher's Acknowledgements
With many thanks to Catherine Ward, Maggi McCormick Gordon, Ingrid Lock, Coral Mula, Kate Simunek and Matthew Ward for all their help.

The thread painting *Golden Angel* (pages 120–3), is reproduced with kind permission of Riki Deardon.

IllustratedLibrary.com

PLEASE NOTE

The images in this book have been proofed to the highest quality possible. However, it should be remembered that colour correction is subjective and open to individual interpretation. The colours reproduced in this book should be used as a guide only – they cannot be used as a completely accurate representation.

The watercolour paints used by the author are manufactured by Winsor & Newton. Similar colours are also available from other paint manufacturers.

The author uses a variety of threads from different manufacturers. DMC embroidery thread colours have been suggested for the projects as the closest representation of her original work.